Longman Self-help Guides

Self-help Groups

Getting started; keeping going

Judy Wilson

Longman

Longman Group UK Limited,
Longman House, Burnt Mill, Harlow,
Essex CM20 2JE, England
and Associated Companies throughout the world.

© Judy Wilson 1986
All rights reserved; no part of this publication
may be reproduced, stored in a retrieval system,
or transmitted in any form or by any means, electronic,
mechanical, photocopying, recording, or otherwise,
without the prior written permission of the Publishers.

First published 1986

British Library Cataloguing in Publication Data
   Wilson, Judy Self-help groups: getting started, keeping
   going.—(Longman self-help guides)
   1. Self-help groups—Great Britain
   I. Title
   361.7   HV245

ISBN 0-582-89268-6

Set in Linotron Plantin by
Tradespools Ltd, Frome, Somerset

Printed in Great Britain
by Mackays, Chatham, Kent

Contents

To Dick

Acknowledgements

I have had a great deal of help in preparing and writing this guide. While the opinions in it are mine, and I take responsibility for the advice, I could not have written it without so much assistance. I would like to thank most warmly everyone who has helped me.

Many members of self-help groups, from whom I have learnt so much, will not know how much they have helped me, but I would like to thank them a great deal.

I owe a lot to the individuals who read drafts and discussed ideas: Irene Bell, Sharon Bryan, Sherry Cook, Eve Cole, Tina Colvin, Shirley Duddy, Peter Durrant, Pat Firman, Liz Haggard, Noreen Miller, Celia Smith, Jill Vincent and Dick Wilson. The librarians of the Volunteer Centre and the National Council for Voluntary Organisations were also most generous with their advice and access to their shelves. I thank them all for their invaluable contributions.

Lastly I would like to thank my colleagues in the Nottingham Self-Help Team, my friends and my family – Clare, Jonathan and Dick – for their support; and last, but far from least, Vera Brooks for her excellent typing.

Judy Wilson

January 1986

Introduction

Starting and running a self-help group is like going on a journey. This guide aims to help you get there. The places you pass through, the route you take, the way you travel and the people you go with – these are your decisions. You'll find I don't try to map out your exact route. There is no one way to start and run a self-help group, but it is helpful to hear about other people's journeys. This guide draws on the experience of many self-help groups and is a combination of practical advice and an account of how self-help groups can best work. This is based on my own personal experience of working with groups and that of the groups themselves.

Have you got a problem yourself, or in your family? Do you want to get together with people in the same situation? Then this book is for you. It is written for people who are, or who are going to be, members of self-help groups. You may never have done anything like this before, and you may be uncertain about what to do and how to do it. I hope I can help you decide which route to take and find some people to travel with – and reassure you that other people have done it before.

Others may find the guide useful too. Are you a professional worker, working with people in self-help groups? This book is not written for you, but you will find it helps you learn more about such groups.

Self help is a way of tackling lots of issues in life, and lies behind many community groups. Here I'm talking to people in a particular kind of self-help group: one based on a personal problem or situation. It could be a health problem, a serious illness or a handicap. It could be a personal situation that leaves you feeling isolated and uncertain. Or some sudden impact on your life, like bereavement, may have left you wanting to get together with people who've gone through it too. This guide may be useful to people in other self-help groups, but it's aimed at people in this particular sort of group. Perhaps 'mutual support groups' is a better way of describing them.

You can have fun on a journey. As you read the guide you'll find ways of tackling some of the issues facing self-help groups. But you needn't be too serious all the time. Self-help groups should have a place for fun and friendship – I hope you get ideas for achieving these too.

Writing a national guide is not easy. Not all the ideas and people suggested here will apply to you, and the names of organizations will vary according to where you live. Not all the advice offered will apply to you and you won't necessarily want to read it all at once. Use it to dip in and out of as it suits you, as you'd use a guidebook on a journey. Use what feels right for you and your group.

Self-help groups are important. They may offer an alternative to professional care, but more often are complementary to the help you may already be getting. I, personally, see self-help groups as a way of strengthening our welfare state, not replacing it. But they are not easy to run. This guide will help you see the issues you need to face, and give you ideas on how to tackle them.

Before you start

What *is* a self-help group?

Before you start, stop and think about self-help groups. First, what exactly *is* a self-help group?

At the root of every self-help group there is a common problem or condition, a common experience or situation. This guide looks particularly at groups based on a serious personal problem. It may even be a life and death situation, and is often a condition needing long-term treatment or a change in life style. It may also be a problem which brings difficulties, not only to the person experiencing it, but to their families and friends as well – and to the community at large. Lack of understanding by other people and a feeling of stigma can make a problem even more difficult to handle.

This is one key idea about self-help groups. This common bond is more than a shared interest. Compare, say, a rose growers' association or a bowls club with a self-help group for relatives of people with senile dementia. In the first, people are drawn together by a common enthusiasm, in the second by a real bond because of their serious common problem.

Another key idea is that *people in groups take on some responsibility for coping with their own problems.* 'I had a lot of help from the doctors, from my family and the church', Janet said when talking about her reaction to having cancer diagnosed. 'But I felt I had to do something for myself too.' People in self-help groups are prepared to do something for themselves. It may well be in addition to professional care or it may be because they are seeking an alternative to the health and social services.

3

Self-help groups are based on *principles of sharing and working co-operatively*. 'There's a strength you can get from other people,' was Margaret's view – her problem was anorexia. People in groups want to work together, not just tackle their problem on their own. Margaret was quite overwhelmed with the support she immediately got from being part of a group facing the same problem. Self-help groups need not be large, 'Two – that's all you need. The others will come', a member of Al-Anon, a group for relatives of people with a drinking problem, told me once. Most are bigger than that, but the ideas of sharing and co-operation are basic to all groups.

A further key idea relates to the reasons behind people's membership. *Most people basically go to self-help groups to meet their own needs, and members should benefit from groups' activities.* 'I go simply for myself', said an AA (Alcoholics Anonymous) member. Jane, a member of a widows' group, went to get help for herself too, but added 'It helped me get over my own bereavement when I suddenly found I was being useful to other people who were worse than me'.

People probably go to and form groups for a variety of reasons, but there is usually an essentially 'selfish' motive behind many people's membership. This is not selfishness in an unpleasant way – it is based on recognition of the need to meet one's own needs. Most groups, in response to this, set up services and activities to benefit the people who actually become members, not all the people in the community who might be interested.

But it's difficult to disentangle motives, and other people, especially if they are over the worst of their problem, may well go largely to be helpful. Like Jane, they get satisfaction from helping other people currently facing the situation. It's sometimes difficult to separate the two motives and indeed one of the wonderful things about a self-help group is that you don't need a label. You are a group member – not a client or a patient, nor a volunteer – sometimes receiving, sometimes giving help. And giving the help can often make you feel better too.

One more key idea: who actually runs a self-help group? Who can join? *People with the problem themselves* – or their relatives, if that is who the group is for – *should decide on its structure, activities and membership*. They should decide too whether to look for or accept outside help. 'We felt we wanted to take responsibility for the group ourselves,' reflected Pete and Sue, both with severe physical handicaps. 'It was difficult to do it all, but important that people didn't do good to us, if you know what we mean.' This doesn't mean that outsiders can't be useful to groups, but group members are right to see the group as theirs.

Of course, not all groups may grow to this pattern. These key ideas may help pull together the common characteristics of self-help groups but there are no rules to which you must conform.

In summary

Self-help groups often share these characteristics:

- A common problem or experience.

- Members join to meet their own needs.

- Members want to take on some responsibility for themselves.

- Members work together to run the group.

The first steps to take

The people quoted in Chapter 1 had all found something for themselves in their self-help group. But just because you have a problem, do you automatically need a self-help group? Do they all work? Is it easy to set one up? In fact, most people with a problem probably don't feel the need to get together with others. Not all groups work, and it is quite difficult to set one up – and even more difficult to keep it going.

It's helpful to begin with a blend of belief in self help and its enormous benefits, mixed with realism, caution and an awareness of the difficulties you might face. Perhaps you might like to regard setting up a group as an experiment. You can find out what is involved, have a try, and abandon the idea if it doesn't work. A course, a radio programme or something similar may have already brought you together with people in a similar situation. But if you are starting from scratch, the following may help you to take the first steps.

Find out if a group already exists which meets your needs

Self-help groups are not always very visible – there might well be a group in your area already in operation. If it gives you what you want, then you may decide to join it and put your energies and time into being a member of an existing group, rather than into setting up a new one. Or you may still decide to go ahead and start your own.

★   Jenny had several members in her immediate family who suffered from severe asthma. She needed information and support herself and had ideas on useful activities for asthma sufferers. She located a local asthma group and travelled over to the south side of the city to go to its daytime meetings. It was a positive, helpful group, but it didn't meet all Jenny's needs. She wanted something more local, evening meetings and activities such as swimming. She discussed the idea of a north city group with the southerners and went away with their support and possible plans for occasional joint meetings.

In Jenny's case, she discovered the group reasonably easily, found it compatible but that it was not local enough – nor did it meet all her needs. A second group based on a common condition in a big city was an obvious solution.

So think about joining an established group as an option. It may in fact suit you more than starting a new one. First though, find your self-help group. Be prepared for a bit of detective work.

Use the phone

You may find using a phone particularly useful, especially if you are not very mobile. Visits may drain your time and energy and there may be queues and waits at even the most friendly offices. If phoning is difficult, you may prefer to write. In this case, be prepared for delays or even no answers.

Where can you enquire?

CONTACT POINTS

Try the following local organizations or people – some at least are likely to exist in your area:

CHECKLIST

- Council for Voluntary Service (CVS) also called Council for Voluntary Action
- Community Council or Rural Community Council
- DIAL (Disablement Information Advice Line)
- Community Health Council (CHC)/Local Health Council/ District Committee
- Citizens Advice Bureau
- Community Relations Council
- Local council information department
- Libraries
- Volunteer Bureau
- Health Education Unit
- Health centres
- MIND (or Association for Mental Health)
- Clergy
- Local newspapers
- The Samaritans
- GPs
- Community nurses
- Health visitors
- Community workers
- Community centres
- Social workers
- Local radio stations

- Women's centres/clinics
- Probation officers
- Council for the Disabled

If you have problems locating this sort of organization, the following suggestions may help:

Use existing contacts that you may have already.

Use the telephone directory and Yellow Pages.

- Local authorities – district and county councils, and in Scotland, regional councils are listed under the name of the council, then the name of the department, then maybe a section of the department.

- Health authorities may be listed under 'Health' or the name of the authority. In England and Wales they are District Health Authorities. In Scotland they are Health Boards, in Northern Ireland, Health and Social Service Boards.

- Councils for Voluntary Service etc. are usually listed under the name of the area first.

- *Yellow Pages* have sections headed 'Charitable and benevolent organisations' and 'Social service and welfare organisations'.

Try and locate local directories

e.g. Directories of local voluntary organizations and social services
Thomsons Directories
Directories produced by newspapers

SPECIAL SELF-HELP CENTRES

In some areas of the country there are now local support and information centres especially for self-help groups. If you have one of these, you will not only get information but extensive help and advice, geared specially for you.

NATIONAL ORGANIZATIONS

There may be a national organization who can tell you if they have a local branch or contact in your area. Look in national directories which are listed on pages 145–6. Your local library will probably have such a directory, which will give details of established national self-help organizations.

Even the most exhaustive detective work may not result in your finding an established group. Or you may find one, and decide you still want to go ahead and form your own. In either case, you'll probably have picked up some useful information, contacts and possible resources on the way, so the detection exercise won't have been wasted. So what's the next step?

Stop and think

Stop and think whether you really want to start a group. Don't worry about if you will be able to, but ask yourself if you *really* want to. Don't underestimate yourself. Even if you've never done anything like this before, you'll be surprised at what you are capable of. But do stop and consider the whole matter.

★ Liz was already a member of an organization based on a common problem, diabetes. It ran though as a rather formal voluntary organization and only met infrequently. Liz wanted a small, mutual support group, meeting more often to help her cope with everyday living. Her job had given her experience, and confidence in organizing but she was anxious about whether she could manage time for a group. What about her health? What did her family think? Would the group all come to depend on her? She took thinking time over several months and emerged with the support of her family and a realistic commitment of her time and energy. Her health was less predictable, but she was willing to take the risk here.

CHECKLIST

● Have you got some spare time? You may not need a lot, but you should have some space in your life in the coming, say, 12 months.

● What do members of your family and close friends think?

- Can you cope with intrusion into your home, by people or the telephone?

- Can you face other people's problems as well as your own?

- Are you well enough? – at least sometimes.

- Are you mobile? It need not stop you starting a group, but you'll need to think through the implication.

- Have you got a telephone? This needn't stop you either, but you'll need to think of ways of managing without one.

- Can you cope with the challenge? It needn't – and probably shouldn't – all depend on you, but a group will make demands on you: emotional, financial and physical as well as taking up your time.

You should also think of all the positive results that could come from starting a self-help group. Your life might change completely. You're more than likely to get at least some help with your own problem. You'll make new friends. You may get busy and fulfilled. And you may discover talents and skills within yourself you never dreamt you had.

So, stop and weigh it up. Think of the year ahead and whether you can put your energy and commitment into a group for that length of time. If you can't, then it may be better to shelve the idea – for good, or maybe until your life or other circumstances change.

Remember that the group won't be just you, of course – it'll be several people working together.

Find some like-minded people

★ Janet was already quite ill by the time she decided to form a cancer group. It was essential for her to find other cancer sufferers who could work with her in setting up a group. She first found Ruth, through a local radio station's phone-in programme. Other like-minded people were put in touch with them through friends and through the CVS, to form a first planning group.

A self-help group cannot be a one-person show, however energetic or experienced they are. It's a positive coming together of several people with the same problem. While you do need to make a personal commitment, you shouldn't be alone. You can start a group with two people but up to about five is a good number to begin planning with, and gives a stronger base.

It may take a little time to identify what you have in common. The like-mindedness won't only apply to the common problem you are all facing, but to the general approach you have to tackling it. A group which decides only to fund-raise for research, or campaign for change is different from a group whose main object is mutual support. If mutual support or information is your initial need, make this clear when you are casting around for your first co-founders.

You may also need to look for people who are in a similar position to yourself. A group of parents of pre-school handicapped children, for example, may have more in common with each other – even if the handicaps are different – than with parents of handicapped teenagers.

How can you find your like-minded people? Go back to the checklist on page 7 – would any of these agencies or people be of use? Word of mouth is a good way of linking people together. Consider too some modest publicity – but a word of warning here. Making time for careful planning can be very fruitful in helping a stable, effective group to emerge. Too much publicity too early can bring large numbers of potential members together too soon, before the group can cope. Be particularly careful how you approach the media at this stage.

Examples of modest publicity could be:

- Handwritten cards or notices in your local library, newsagent, corner shop, health food shop or book shop.

- An advertisement in the personal column of the local paper, using a Box number or a friendly organization's address.

- A note in church magazines or weekly newssheets.

- A poster in a hospital outpatients' waiting area or a surgery or health centre – ask for their agreement first.

Each area will have its own opportunities and you can probably think of many others in your neighbourhood.

Get together

There's more than one way to make links, of course. Your first contact might well be individually by phone or letter. Or you may start with a big public meeting, even if you didn't actually plan it that way. Self-help groups don't grow steadily or predictably.

If you can control the group's growth a bit, then it's well worth thinking about getting your first few like-minded people together for a chat. Have several small meetings if you feel you need them – plenty of planning and thinking together is likely to pay off in the end.

You have a choice of where you meet at this stage: first, numbers will probably be small enough to meet in someone's home. The advantages here are that it will be free, comfortable, friendly and warm. But you may prefer a neutral meeting place. Going to someone else's house can sometimes be difficult.

If there is not an obvious room in a house, or people really do prefer to meet in a neutral place, then ask around for a free room for a couple of meetings. Many of the organizations listed in the checklist on page 7 might be willing to help, particularly the CVS or CHC. But don't accept the offer of a cold room, seating a hundred on hard chairs – that could actually prevent your group getting off the ground.

★   Pat and Richard were lucky. In their town, there was a self-help groups' support project that lent them a small room for their first planning meetings. Richard's main anxiety was his fear that a group would come to depend on him; Pat's that her home would be invaded. Both were suffering from migraine, an unpredictable condition that made their regular attendance questionable. Four small meetings were held over a three-month period in which these problems were aired and they got to know each other. In particular, they spent a lot of time discussing the purpose of a group and the jobs to be done in setting it up. All members of the initial group were emphatic that they didn't want to have sole responsibility and ways of sharing the jobs out was a topic that they looked at in depth.

What could you discuss in these informal meetings? You'll probably find you want to look at:

Membership Is the group going to be just for people with the problem? Are their relatives welcome as well or do you in fact need two groups? Are you going to allow interested people – 'sympathizers' – to come too, or will this dilute the purpose of the group? What about professional workers?

Size Groups can vary from two to 200. Their size is related to many factors, including the incidence of the problem and the objectives of the group. If you decide your prime objective is mutual support through discussion, for example, then a membership of 10 to 20 is probably reasonable. Don't be too ambitious about members, or get anxious if they appear to be few.

Objectives Self-help groups can undertake all sorts of activities. What do you want out of the group at first? You'll find you need not only to talk through the overall, maybe long-term objectives, but also priorities within them. It's wise not to be over-ambitious at first.

By the time you have tackled these and other topics, you may find you have a group already, particularly if you decide on a small membership. In this case your next challenge is making it work, rather than going public. Often however, once people have talked through the issues in a small group, they decide to become more visible, to go public and widen their membership.

Plan an initial meeting

While someone's front room may work well for planning meetings, or for very small local groups, most groups will benefit from using a public building of some kind. It allows anonymity, a neutral base, continuity and flexibility.

As well as deciding on this, you'll need to consider the time of year. It's amazing how a combination of holiday periods and bad weather can restrict the available months: spring, early summer and early autumn are generally good times for a launch. Time of day, and day of the week need to be considered too. Avoid Mondays for regular meetings because of Bank Holidays.

Two more important matters are the availability of any speaker you decide to have; and the possibility of getting a free meeting room. Sometimes flexibility over dates can help you get a rent-free room or an important speaker. It can be quite a juggling act.

Eventually you'll end up with a date, a time and a room. What other decisions do you need to make? The checklist below may be helpful:

CHECKLIST

- Who is going to welcome people at the door?

- Are you having a speaker? Will he or she be local, or maybe from a national organization? For how long will they speak? On what topic? What equipment might be needed and who will test it beforehand? Who will brief the speaker? How long should they stay? Will they need a meal – if so, where and when?

- Would you prefer a video film? Who will provide and test the equipment?

- Who is going to chair the meeting? What will they be responsible for – don't be afraid to work it out together, especially if you haven't done it before.

- Arrangements for tea and coffee. When? Where? How much will it cost? How many cups? Who is going to wash up?

- Attendance list – are you going to ask people to give their names and addresses? If so, when and where? Or is anonymity better?

- How long will the meeting last? What should be the balance between informal and formal chat? How can the time be used most fruitfully? Will the caretaker eject you?

- Money. Are you going to ask for donations? Who, if so, will look after the money?

- Are you going to wear labels?

- Who is going to arrange the chairs and put them back as you found them? How do you want them arranged?

- Are there access, parking and toilets for people with disabilities? Can you mention that on your publicity material?

- Is there a loudspeaker system – and maybe a loop system for people with hearing aids? Who will check it is working?

At the same time as planning the first meeting, start thinking in your planning group about a second. If the first one is successful, people will want to know, on the spot, when they can meet again. It's worth guessing among you what might be an acceptable date and place, and making a provisional booking of the same, or another room.

A blackboard, or a large sheet of paper on the wall, in your initial meeting room can be useful for writing up the details of the next meeting – particularly if the meeting is large or people have hearing problems. Announce it well before the end of the formal part of the evening, when people can begin to drift away.

Allow an informal time at the end. People simply enjoy talking, but a first meeting of a self-help group can be a profoundly moving experience, and they will need time to unwind before going home.

In summary

- Find out if there is a group already, and if there is, try it out.

- Stop and think.

- Find some like-minded people.

- Get together.

- Plan an initial meeting.

Membership and activities

You should ask yourself three questions: Who will be members of your group? What do you want to achieve? What activities could you undertake? Group members need to share responsibility, and should not look to and depend on one key figure. Considering these questions together gives a good opportunity for all the early members of an embryo group to be involved.

The more specific you can be about membership, and the more precise about the group's purpose, the more likely it is to succeed – so it's worth giving ample time to thinking about and discussing both. Decisions about activities will then emerge more easily.

Who will be members?

In your search for a few like-minded people you may already have had to come to some tentative conclusions. One example is a situation where you personally are sure that you only want to get together with people who have direct experience of your problem. This means you will not be inviting either your relatives or other people's families to become members of the group. You will need to accept that defining membership will inevitably require you to exclude some people – don't feel guilty about this. Some of the most successful groups are those who are very specific about who can join.

FAMILIES

But it may not always be appropriate for the boundaries of membership to be drawn too tight. Often people feel that attending a group with their partner is one way of understanding and coming to terms with their problem together. Sometimes whole families – for example those with one child who is handicapped and others who are able bodied – may get immense benefit from attending. Whatever is decided, make it known through your publicity material as to who is invited.

SYMPATHIZERS

It's not only other members of the family you have to consider.
What about 'sympathizers' as one group called them? This group
specifically welcomed sympathizers to their meetings and this may
have been one of the reasons why this group didn't last very long.
It had the effect of diluting the group to a general interest group,
rather than one with a strong common bond. You'll need to make
your own decision on this. One way round it is to opt for occasional
open meetings, maybe with a speaker, when anyone can come. Or
you can ask outsiders to help at a fund-raising event or project.

PROFESSIONALS

What about professionals? Where someone shares the problem and
happens to be a professional – a social worker with a physical
handicap, for example – then of course there will be no exclusion.
In fact their skills and experience may come in very useful as long
as they are offered as an ordinary group member. Most groups will
probably evolve methods for linking and support from other
professionals where this seems appropriate, rather than having
them as members.

Membership

Here are some questions which it may be useful to consider:

- Are you going to require subscriptions?

- What happens if people don't pay? Do they stop being
  members?

- Will they need to become members of a national organization
  in order to go to a local branch?

- Will members need to make some commitment? For example,
  agreeing with the objectives of the group.

- Will they be required to attend regularly?

- Must they take on some task, and if so, straight away, or later?

There are unlikely to be quick answers to all these questions –
membership will probably evolve with the group. Who should be
members will probably be one of the first issues you tease out with

your like-minded people. In fact, it can be a good issue for everyone to go away and do a bit of work on. You can use different people as sounding boards and draw from the experience of other groups. While you may not want to rush decisions on membership, don't take too long to come to an agreement on limits.

Whatever your conclusions you'll probably decide that members should have a *common bond*. This could be:

- A similar problem

- A common feeling or outlook

- A particular characteristic in common or perhaps a combination of two or all of these.

Some groups ask too for some personal *commitment* – AA, for example, from whom newer groups can learn a great deal, ask that people should have a desire to stop drinking.

Some groups also ask people to try and build in a commitment to *attendance*. It's wise however to be relaxed about this, especially as so many people will have problems that make regular attendance uncertain. Most groups have an open door policy, and accept that many people will come in and out. But bear in mind that many of the more established groups have a hard core of regular attenders. This can be an important element in the success of a self-help group, though it takes time to achieve.

What do you want to achieve?

You may think this is self-evident once you have decided on membership. It's all too easy though for people to assume there is agreement over what the group is about, and to coast along without clarifying specific aims. Being specific can definitely contribute to success – it's another matter worth discussing.

You need to decide what the goals, objectives and priorities of the group are to be.

Goals are the overall aims of the group – and only you and your fellow members can determine these. Even if groups in different towns share the same problem, the goals they set themselves may be very different. If you are setting up a local branch of a national organization, however, you may need to take on their goals in order to qualify for affiliation. National organizations are often very definite about goals for local branches.

Objectives are the smaller and more precise aims the group sets itself in order to reach a goal. They may vary over time, and change as the group changes. You are unlikely to be able to work on them all at once, so you will need to set priorities.

Priorities will probably evolve as compromises between various points of view of group members. They should not be woolly compromises – more a realistic way of appreciating that the group will probably want to do a lot of things and that people's views will differ on what should be done first. It's better not to be too ambitious at first. If you are successful in a small way it will be a great boost to morale. While if you are too confident about what is possible initially it can actually destroy the group.

Decisions on goals, objectives, priorities and membership could be made by group leaders. They could simply tell the members of the group what is going to be done. It does happen. But if you want most members of the group to share in its running, then participation must come at this stage too.

Achieving participation and making decisions democratically will not be easy and will take some time. Evolve a way that suits you, the numbers in the group and the room you meet in. Don't forget to take account of any particular handicap which might inhibit participation – hearing loss or visual handicap, for example. Consider whether members of your group are happiest talking or writing. Here are some possible ways of getting discussion going.

Encourage people to join in

Threesomes If you have between 10 and 20 people at a meeting, divide them into threes. Get them to sit in different parts of the room and spend half an hour discussing what they feel about the group, and what they want from it. Put a large sheet of paper up on the wall, get everyone together again and ask each group to contribute points that came up. Use large felt-tipped pens and write their ideas on the paper. At your next meeting, put the sheet up again and use it to help you come to some decisions about the group.

Questionnaires Some groups have had 100 or more people at their inaugural meeting. Short questionnaires about what people want from a group could be the solution when large numbers are expected. Get them typed and duplicated beforehand. It's probably best to ask people to hand them in at the end of the meeting. Otherwise, put an address on them, and a date by which they should be returned. Decide in advance who is going to analyse the replies, and fix a date for the steering group to discuss the results.

Making time Small groups don't need to have any special ways of getting people involved. But at the beginning of a group, people can be so engrossed in their own problem – and so relieved to find others with whom to share it – that there is no time to discuss issues affecting the group. This situation demands making time in a meeting, or deciding to spend a particular meeting discussing group issues rather than personal situations.

What is feasible to achieve?

When you have got some way to deciding on what you would like to achieve, you'll also need to give some thought as to what is feasible. The two will probably be interwoven in your discussions. Not all you'd like to do will be possible. You'll need to take into account, for example:

- Your members' situations

- The size of your active membership

- The attitude of professionals and the community towards you

- What resources you have initially.

★   A new group in a country area decided that mutual support through talking was high on their list of priorities. Ideally, they would have liked to meet frequently but transport and lack of a central meeting place made this difficult. But they found that everyone was on the phone. They decided to set up a system for phone contact, and for letter writing to complement occasional meetings.

A group taking this sort of approach is being realistic. When you consider what activities you could undertake, think realistically, concentrating on what is feasible, and what strategies you could adopt to help you achieve your aims. Ask yourselves:

- What is right for us?

- What is feasible?

- How fast can we move?

What activities could your group undertake?

REGULAR MEETINGS

There are very few groups who do not have regular meetings – most people find they want this as a hard core of their activities, and for some groups, it's almost their only formal activity. Face to face contact, sharing in a group, making the effort to get out – these all seem to contribute to a self-help group helping people with their problems. What actually happens in a meeting will vary. It could include:

- Sharing experiences

- Giving mutual support

- Passing on information

- Planning other activities

Alcoholics Anonymous have evolved a particular way of running meetings. There is a simple, but definite, format which gives older members the chance to tell their story, and for newcomers to take part if they want. It also means that anyone can chair the meeting. It may be helpful to visit AA even if you decide to organize your meetings very differently.

Many AA groups have occasional open meetings and you might find it useful to sit in on one. The national address is on page 147 if you can't easily locate a branch near you.

PROVIDING INFORMATION, ADVICE, AND PERSONAL
SUPPORT

The need for *information*, sometimes to the point of desperation, is
a very common need in people in self-help groups. Groups can
often be a very useful source of help. This can be provided by:

- Asking people with specialist knowledge to give a talk.

- Compiling a library of relevant books and articles.

- Producing literature.

- Knowing other useful sources of help.

Professionals are sometimes concerned that self-help groups will
hand out inaccurate advice. Work out what sort of information you
can give and don't go beyond it. Many groups based on health
problems make it clear that they don't provide medical advice, and
instead encourage people to return to professional workers.

Personal support will probably evolve naturally in your group
meetings, in friendships outside the group and in telephone calls.
This may be enough. In some groups however, established
members of the group befriend newcomers, who are then offered
the opportunity of personal one-to-one support, as in the following
example.

★   A group for widows and widowers recognized the need for
     people to have personal befriending, especially soon after their
     bereavement. But they also felt that it was a difficult job to do
     well. A professional counsellor was drawn in to run a 6-week
     course for some of the members on befriending and being a
     good listener. The group now offers a link with one of these as
     part of its service of support. Members in turn have grown in
     confidence and skills, and enjoy being able to participate more
     fully in one of the group's activities.

PROVIDING SERVICES

Many groups decide that they can't get what they need from
existing services and that they will run their own. A word of
caution: it can be all too easy to define a need and rush to fill it.
Think through this checklist before starting a service.

CHECKLIST

- Is the service being provided elsewhere already?

- Could this existing service meet members' needs, as it is, or with some modest changes?

- How much will it cost? Who will pay?

- What will be essential for it to succeed? Will it need transport, for example?

- Who will be able to use the service? Members only? Anyone in need? How many people?

- What priority should it have in your activities?

- Is lease of a building involved?

- Would campaigning for someone else to provide the service be a better use of your time?

- Could launching a service stop your group giving enough time for mutual support through talking?

Crack – the group for multiple sclerosis sufferers – provides an example of a successful service.

★ A large local branch decided that the need for exercise – a key thing for MS sufferers – could be met best by a weekly class for its members. They recruited a physiotherapist and volunteer helpers and booked a hall with suitable equipment. Members enthuse about its benefits and enjoy seeing each other outside the monthly meetings.

SOCIAL ACTIVITIES

Don't feel you have to have these as a matter of course. Sometimes social activities are best when spontaneous, informal and outside the normal pattern of meetings. But some organized events can contribute to maintaining the momentum of a self-help group. You'll know best what works for you, but keep it simple and cheap to start with, and have something that doesn't depend on large numbers. Not everyone will come. Here are some examples of successful social events groups have run:

- A country walk
- A children's party
- A film show
- A square dance
- A meal in a restaurant
- Theatre visits
- A museum visit
- A coffee evening
- An outing to London
- A canal trip

Be careful that social activities will add to – not detract from – your overall goals, and when they are planned bear in mind both the condition on which the group is based and on what people can afford.

FUND-RAISING

Some groups fund-raise, others don't at all. For a few it is their main aim. What are your reasons for fund-raising? How much do you want to raise in a year? Who will benefit from the money? These are some of the questions you'll need to ask yourselves. Many groups find it another way of consolidating the group and having an enjoyable time. Other groups use it as a vital tool for campaigning for change. Some groups overdo fund-raising so that it becomes a burden and puts members off, rather than drawing them in.

Here's an example of a group who undertook fund-raising as a positive and enjoyable exercise, clearly related to the group's goals. Raising money proved an essential tool for the changes that have now taken place.

★   A local branch of parents who had had a stillborn child decided that one of their aims was to get the local hospital to change the way parents were dealt with at this distressing time. After their fund-raising efforts they gave the hospital beautiful baby clothes and a camera (so that the child could be photographed) and a book of remembrance, and furnished a parents' room. They used quite ordinary methods – holding jumble sales (some at the hospital) and selling Christmas cards – to considerable success.

CAMPAIGNING

You and your group will know at first hand just what it is like to live with your problem, and what helps you cope with it. If you feel you want to tell people who plan and provide services how you feel about them, then go ahead and do so. This doesn't necessarily mean a banner-waving demonstration – the actual method of campaigning will depend on you, and on your relationships with professionals and politicians. Sometimes they may actually approach you, as one doctor did when wanting reaction to the way his clinic was run.

It is more difficult to feed back experience as a consumer in the health and social services than in say, your local supermarket. Individuals are understandably reluctant to appear to criticize helpful professionals, and are often vulnerable and lacking confidence because of their problem. A group however can take up issues, quietly or loudly, to let professionals and policy-makers know its views.

One new group successfully campaigned on one issue, getting considerable publicity for their overall activities in the process.

★ The secretary of a new branch of the Partially Sighted Society heard a journalist advise groups to find an issue which would interest the media, if they want publicity. The group was most concerned at the time at the plan to charge for phone calls to Directory Enquiries. They wrote letters, sent copies to the press and ended up on the front page of the local paper three nights running – and 14 nights running inside. The paper itself in fact took up their cause. The publicity about the group helped boost the group's confidence and brought in many new members. The plan to charge everyone for enquiries was quietly dropped.

In summary

- Be specific about membership and be precise about your goals.

- Take time to consider both and involve as many people as you can in making decisions about them.

- Consider carefully what activities you want to undertake.

- Be careful not to be too ambitious at first.

Facing practical issues

Rooms for meetings

Getting the right room for your meetings is very important. If it is a good place, you will find your meetings run much better, are more enjoyable and, most important, people are more likely to come.

Do you belong to any other organizations? Where do they hold their meetings? Do you like the meeting room? Could you find it on your first visit? Do you find it easy to get to? If the answers are no, did you ever feel resentment, maybe grumbled about it? This exercise may help in planning the sort of place where the new self-help group should meet.

Meeting rooms may prove to be a particularly difficult issue for groups in rural areas. There is likely to be less choice of rooms, there may be no obvious central place and transport must be considered alongside decisions on where to meet.

Wherever you live, you'll need to bear the following points in mind when choosing your meeting place:

- The character of the room, particularly how welcoming it feels.

- How comfortable it is – and accessible.

- The chairs available, and how they are arranged.

- Car-parking.

- Coffee and tea arrangements.

- Caretakers.

Early meetings

Don't worry too much about getting it all right in the early stages. When you are having early planning meetings, your numbers are likely to be small, people will be well motivated and there is bound to be personal contact before a meeting. It will be relatively easy to explain where it is being held and what travel arrangements are best.

You will probably be most concerned to get a room quickly, and somewhere free. You may find that someone's house is perfectly suitable. If you have a Council for Voluntary Service or Community Council near you, it is very likely that they can let you have a small, free room for a few sessions. Part of their job is to help people when starting up. But look back through the checklist on page 7. Other organizations, especially if you have a personal contact, may also be worth approaching. Explain it is only a temporary arrangement.

You will need privacy. Meeting in a coffee bar or a pub won't do – people may well want to talk about their personal needs.

Part of the task of your planning group will be to make arrangements for rooms for regular meetings. It's a job that can be shared out – don't do it all yourself. What do you need to think about?

Regular meetings

What you take into account will depend on your particular group, any disability members may have, and where you live. You may find it helpful to run through this next checklist together and pick out the points that apply to you.

CHECKLIST

- Is the atmosphere welcoming?
- Is the meeting place centrally located, within easy reach of the town, your neighbourhood or a group of villages?
- Is the building easy to find from the street?
- Will you need to send a map?

- Is the room easily identifiable when you get in the building?

- Can you put up notices about your meeting?

- Is the room accessible for anyone with a physical handicap? (Think about this even if your group is not based on a physical disability). Are there toilets and ramps for the disabled?

- Is there a loop system for people with hearing loss?

- Is the meeting place near a public transport route?

- Is there parking? Is it near enough the entrance for people with a physical handicap?

- Will the room seat the number of people you expect?

- What time of day, and which day of the week is best?

- Is there room for any activities? (e.g. small discussion groups).

- Are the chairs all the same height? (It helps discussion if they are).

- Are the chairs suitable? (e.g. A young people's group may prefer cushions and a carpet; back pain sufferers will appreciate hard upright chairs).

- Is there anything about the building or the room which could bring distress or difficulty to people, because of their personal problem?

- Can you arrange the seating as you want?

- Can you make, or get, tea and coffee at a time that suits you?

- Is the building noisy? Or will it be when your meeting is held?

- Is it warm? (More important than you might think.)

- Do you need a blackboard or flip chart?

- Is smoking allowed, and if so, are ashtrays provided?

- Are you allowed to hold raffles?

- What does it cost to hire?

- Must you book a series of meetings in advance?

- What are the caretaking arrangements?
- What is the latest time by which you must leave?

There is a lot to think about. In a big city, you'll probably have a lot of choice. In the country, you may have very little. Finding a suitable room can be very challenging for people in the country. Don't hesitate to ask for help from outside bodies if it begins to feel too daunting. You are of course unlikely to find a room that meets all your requirements. You may need to settle on a room that is adequate rather than perfect.

And you may find that the room you choose initially is not the one you settle in permanently. Perhaps you have to try it out first, or your numbers change radically, but aim to settle somewhere as soon as possible. It will help give both character and continuity to your group, and will make advertising for new members much easier.

Central sources of information about meeting rooms

Some towns have central sources of information about rooms to let which will save you time and effort. They may be listed in a directory; information may be available in files at an office; or someone may carry useful knowledge in their head. The most likely places to have such a source are:

- The library
- Local council information department
- Council for Voluntary Service
- Community Council

Find out whether any of them have such information. It probably won't be totally up to date, and may not include exact charges, but it will save you time and provide phone numbers to follow up. From this you can produce a short list for members to visit and consider further.

Free rooms

Quite a few self-help groups meet in premises which they get free of charge. Others decide on principle not to accept rent-free accommodation. What are the advantages and disadvantages?

ADVANTAGES	DISADVANTAGES
No rent to find	May not be able to control arrangements
Less fund-raising	
Less financial demand on members	Possible lack of continuity
	May bring group too close to professional care
Improved links with professionals	May be difficult to invite outside 'alternative' speakers
Familiar places easy to find	Caretakers may resent you
	If it is uncomfortable, can you complain?

Think through these issues; three short stories which illustrate them may help.

★ The Monday group welcomed the close link they had developed with hospital social workers, and the way it brought them new members. People were familiar with the hospital and there was much appreciation of the services it provided. The acceptance of the offer of a meeting room there seemed sensible. It brought problems however – a long walk from the entrance; poor signposting; uncertainty about exactly which room could be used; and no control about when the urn of coffee would arrive, if it did at all! The group decided to go for stability and continue to meet there. Some of the difficulties were resolved and they were careful to give good directions to new members.

★ The Thursday group's members had very mixed feelings about hospitals and consultants. Some had actually joined the group after despairing of professional care helping them at all. In no way could the group have met its objectives if it met on health service premises. A member's sitting room, central and with parking near, met their needs for the first year. But secretly the member began to resent using her flat and, as she got better, didn't always want to be at meetings herself. The solution was a comfortable informal room at a community centre, on a bus route, and with access to the kitchen to make drinks as and when they wanted. Small numbers sometimes meant that donations at the meeting didn't always cover the rent, but an occasional fund-raising event provided a subsidy.

★ The Wednesday group knew from the start that their problem meant that fund-raising would be difficult, especially as they had so many other things to do. They were keen to invite speakers on alternative therapies, operating outside the NHS. They had enjoyed joint meetings of self-help groups held in a pleasant modern Social Services Day Centre for the elderly. The warden was anxious to see the building fully used, and negotiated a free letting for them too. The out-of-town location was balanced by good car parking and a most helpful caretaker.

If you decide to investigate using a free room, then don't hesitate to ask. Try any of the following:

CHECKLIST

- GP
- Health visitor
- Hospital social worker
- Area social worker
- Specialist social worker
- Health Centre administrator
- Parish council
- Women's institute
- Schools
- Adult education centre
- Libraries

- Pubs
- Churches
- Community Health Council
- Day Centres

But do think about the consequences first, and come to a clear, written agreement with the owners. You can even build in a review on both sides and set a limit on the length of time the agreement will last. Don't accept being a poor relation – it is better to pay if that seems to be the relationship required by whoever is in charge of the room.

Layout of the room

What are you trying to achieve in your group? How many people will there be? Is there going to be a talk, with slides that everyone must be able to see? The layout of your room is very important in relation to the success of your meetings.

Room layouts

Don't feel you have to accept a room as the previous users left it. Put the chairs and tables in the shape that suits you. A friendly caretaker may even do it for you, but arrive early to make sure they are in the right position, and offer to put them back at the end of the meeting. Get help from able-bodied friends if members would find it difficult.

Most small groups find it is easier to share a problem or ideas if they sit in a circle, quite close to each other. And while they may decide to have a person in the chair, this arrangement prevents the meeting from being dominated. Large groups may have less choice. See whether you can break up the arrangement in any way – perhaps sitting in groups of three or four round a table, all facing the speaker. The principle should be that the room arrangement will enable your meeting to work more effectively.

Caretakers

Helpful, cheerful, go-out-of-their-way-to-help-you caretakers will make all the difference to you. Tired, overworked, grumpy caretakers may make your meeting a disaster.

You may not be able to do much about their basic characters, but you can get to know them. You can thank them for their help. You can give them a Christmas present. Regard them as one of the challenges your group has to face and work out how best to relate to them. This may be especially true for groups getting a free booking.

Insurance

Some groups will want to make sure that they are insured while using the meeting room. If you do, ask the owner of the building what you are covered for through their policy. If the building burns down through the negligence of one of your members, are you covered? Pure accidents will not make you legally liable.

The easiest way to get cover is to ask the owner to extend their policy to make sure it includes you as a user of the building. It may cost you a bit more but may be worth it. It is more expensive to take out your own Public Liability insurance through an insurance firm or a broker. You may also want to consider insurance against loss of people's belongings, but this will probably only apply to established groups, running a range of activities and meeting frequently.

Continuity

There are three good reasons for trying to get a settled satisfactory meeting place:

- The place you meet in will have an atmosphere and character of its own. It's surprising how much this will contribute to the group.

- It's very reassuring for people who are worried to come regularly to the same room, in the same building.

- Publicity to attract new members will be much easier. A change of meeting place will require new publicity material. You will also have to take down old posters and to put a notice up at your old meeting place. You may well lose members through a change.

Leasing a building – or part of it

As some groups grow, they may feel the need for their own place. It may be that they are having frequent meetings or courses; they may need an office base; or they may take on paid staff. Most of this guide is aimed at fairly modest, mutual support groups that won't be taking this step. Self-help groups that move beyond this stage should recognize the different challenges such a change presents them with. Advice from outside may prove particularly useful, and some of the books listed on page 144 will also guide you. Don't rush into the commitment having your own place brings. Think about it carefully, read further and ask for help.

In summary: seven Cs

- Character
- Comfort
- Continuity

- Chairs
- Car-parking
- Coffee
- Caretakers

Think through your needs, evaluate the advantages and disadvantages of possible venues, and be prepared to pay if it means you can meet your needs better.

Money

Your group will need money. But think of people and their needs first, rather than money first. Don't let money, either the lack or the pursuit of it, interfere with what you want your group to do. Rather let it be one of the resources that makes it work. Think particularly of how getting money together fits in with principles of self help and sharing. Make it a positive, bonding experience rather than a drudge.

Groups vary enormously over their attitude to money. Consider these two examples.

FUND-RAISING: A DISTRACTION

★   Alcoholics Anonymous actually turns down offers of money from outside, limits the amount that any one member may contribute and declines help like free meeting rooms. In its twelve traditions, it includes the principles that

'An A.A. group ought never to endorse, finance or lend the A.A. name to any related facility or outside enterprise, lest problems of money, property and prestige divert us from our primary purpose. Every A.A. group ought to be fully self-supporting, declining outside contributions.'

FUND-RAISING: A POSITIVE BOND

★   A village-based group of asthma sufferers, and parents of children with asthma, illustrates the way in which fund-raising provided the core to group activity. The reason for their formation was to raise money to buy nebulizers for GPs to carry in their cars. Use of this equipment, if quickly available, could prevent children's admission to hospital. The group found great satisfaction from doing something so constructive. Through their fund-raising efforts they got to know each other better and talked about their problems.

Both are self-help groups, but their attitude to money is radically different. What will your attitude be? If you are sure that money will be low on your list of priorities, then a quick read through this section may be sufficient. If your group is very interested in money – and what can be done with it – then regard this section only as a signpost, not an exhaustive guide. You will need to seek further guidance, using the lists of books and addresses on pages 144–8.

Money isn't just an issue which self-help groups have to tackle – any new group needs to think about it. You may already have been involved in another organization and if you think back, their experience over funds and fund-raising may provide useful pointers. Self-help groups, though, are a bit different from other voluntary groups. It's worth thinking about your group and its special needs and resources.

Why do you need money?

First, think about it from your situation as a new group. What might you need money for when you begin? These are costs some groups have found they have needed to meet early on:

- Rent of a meeting room
- Duplicating and printing (notices of meetings, headed notepaper, publicity material, members' newsletters)
- Newspaper advertisements about meetings
- Secretary's expenses (phone calls etc.)
- Postage

- Refreshments at meetings
- Speakers' expenses

Some groups, especially those that decide to limit their numbers and to concentrate on mutual support, will never need to move beyond this type of expense. Others however, will grow both in numbers, and in what they want to achieve. This second list includes some of the ways in which groups have spent money once they have become established.

- Providing equipment
- Contributing to research funds
- Setting up a phone-in service
- Employing a worker
- Meeting travel expenses of members who visit housebound fellow members
- Paying travel costs to meetings
- Affiliation fees to national or local organizations
- Putting on a holiday play-scheme
- Establishing a library
- Running outings
- Producing their own publications
- Attending conferences
- Subscribing to specialist journals

Each group will need to agree what it wants to do and the priorities it will set. Your group's attitude to money, the amount you will need and the way you will raise it will depend very much on the overall goals and the specific objectives that you set together.

It is particularly important that the enthusiasm of a single member does not lead the group to commit time and energy to what can be an enormous and exhausting task. Groups have had to disband completely because of over-ambitious fund-raising plans and poor account keeping.

Do you actually have to raise money at all? You need resources, but there are ways of getting some of them without paying.

Free or cheap help

Think about what you want to do. Can you achieve at least some of it if you get help 'in kind'? That is, people don't actually give you money, but give you help or resources without any charge. This list shows what groups have successfully got for free:

- A meeting room
- Duplicating or photocopying
- Use of other people's mailings
- Inclusion in a local newspaper (in a 'What's on' column, a letter or as a news item)
- Donations of equipment
- Equipment bought at a discount through local authorities
- Notepaper printed in a hospital occupational therapy department
- Raffle prizes
- A speaker
- A leader of a training course
- Advertising by firms in publications, reducing printing costs
- A student attached to the group on a placement

There will probably be a lot of goodwill in your community towards your group. Don't be afraid to tap it, if you feel the help is appropriate. Use your contacts, publicize your needs. It may be much better to put a modest amount of energy into this kind of tactic, rather than into straight fund-raising or delving deep into your members' pockets. But you will almost certainly want to acquire some actual money too. There are different ways of getting money both from within the group, and from outside it.

Raising money

Here is a brief summary of six possible methods of getting money.

GETTING MONEY FROM YOUR MEMBERS

Most people coming to a group will accept that they will be contributing to it financially. It's a good idea to get this built in to a group's traditions right at the start because introducing it later on can cause problems. There are a number of ways in which you can arrange this:

- Passing the hat round so each person makes a contribution when they attend.

- A subscription system, annually or otherwise.

- A joining fee.

- Charging extra for tea and coffee, on top of what it actually costs.

- A small raffle at the meeting.

- A bring-and-buy sale at the meeting – plants or home-made food are usually winners.

ORGANIZING FUND-RAISING EVENTS

There are probably at least 100 different events and activities you could consider putting on. It needn't always be a jumble sale, though some groups swear by them. Whatever you do, think through this checklist.

CHECKLIST

- Will it all depend on one person, or can you involve most of the group?

- Will it be fun?

- Will it help you to get to know each other better?

- How big an event is suitable for you?

- Are you risking losing money?

- How much time and planning will it take?

- What image will it give your group?

- Can you put on your event as part of someone else's bigger function?

- How much will it depend on the weather?

- Do you need insurance?

- What is suitable for your members' age, interests and health?

- Do you have enough ablebodied help?

Fund-raising events run by other people

Here's a way to involve 'sympathizers': ask them to put on a fundraising event for you. This next example shows that people may actually also come to you and offer to run an event to benefit your funds.

★ Headline, a group for people with head injuries and their families, gained a large income derived from other people's efforts. A village cricket team challenged them to a match, and with a little help from some well-known county players, Headline won, not only the match, but £800. The same village has an annual pram race, Headline's contribution: ten collectors for two hours. Profit: £935. Lastly, some friendly physiotherapists did a sponsored abseil and gave a major slice of the £2000 receipts to the group.

The scale of success may not apply to you, but consider the principle of asking people sympathetic to your needs to undertake a fund-raising event for you.

GRANTS FROM LOCAL COUNCILS AND HEALTH AUTHORITIES

You may value autonomy and independence and fear that money from this source means you will lose them. But small grants rarely lead to control over your activities. If you decide to go ahead, the following advice may be useful:

- Raise some of the money you need by your own efforts first.

- Think through what to ask for from a particular source.

- Find out if there is an official with particular responsibility for voluntary groups, and ask their advice.

- Follow the procedure the council or health authority has set out for making applications.

- Take time and care with your application, typing it if possible.

- Send copies of your annual accounts and report with your application.

MONEY FROM TRUSTS

This may not be a fruitful source for new, informal groups. One restriction is that most charitable trusts are only able to give money to registered charities. Another limit is scale – over 2400 trusts are listed in the Directory of Grant-making Trusts. However, some self-help groups may benefit by exploring this source. If your group wants to do so, consider the following.

Local charitable trusts A list of local trusts is probably available from your library. The level of grant may be nearer your scale, and your own local emphasis will appeal to them.

Applying for a grant for a specific piece of work While trusts give money both for general activities and for particular projects, they are likely to look with more interest at a request to support a specific interesting piece of work.

Seek further advice if you decide to go ahead with getting money from trusts. Be prepared to do a lot of paper work, and to wait a long time for decisions.

MONEY FROM INDUSTRY

Consider whether this is more appropriate for your group. By far the greatest number of donations from firms are made locally and this again is a strong starting point. Firms like to have a caring image and to build good relations with the local community. They will not be so concerned about charitable status and constitutions. On the other hand, they are less likely to support innovation, or schemes that benefit less attractive minority groups. They like to help 'good causes'. If you feel you can make yourself into a 'good cause', have a go.

Do you have contacts with any of the following?

- Chamber of Commerce
- Junior Chamber of Commerce
- Trades Council
- Individual trades unions
- Action Resource Centre
- Rotary Club or Round Table
- Local large firms

People in these organizations may be valuable sources of advice on where to go and how to focus your appeal. Remember too the suggestions given on getting help in kind. You may find that firms are more likely to donate their products than to give money. It may help to give them a choice between the two.

Fund-raising and the law

If you are largely fund-raising from your members, or undertaking modest, informal fund-raising events, there are no formal legal requirements to which you have to conform. Once you become more ambitious, you will find it easier if you become a registered charity.

Activities which require approval from the local council are:

- House-to-house collections
- Street collections
- Gaming and lotteries (other than small scale gaming and raffles)

Check details with your council, and seek further advice, once you decide to move out of small fund-raising efforts.

Appointing a treasurer

You've thought *why* you need the money, and considered *how* you might get it. Just as important is to consider the *way it should be looked after*. It is essential that even a few pounds belonging to a group is properly accounted for. It's not only your public image that is important here but the feeling of trust and confidence that members of the group have in the way funds are managed. And it's trust that must dictate the appointment of a treasurer.

Do have a treasurer. Other positions of authority can be shared, but you need one person handling and accounting for the money. If amounts are small, no great financial expertise is needed.

What does a treasurer do? The following list (from *Organising your group – notes for treasurers* by Celia Smith, National Childminding Association) provides a quick summary of the job. The treasurer's main duties are to:

- Open a bank account
- Collect any income and issue receipts
- Keep simple accounts of all income and expenditure
- Pay bills
- Report to the group on its financial state
- Prepare and present a balance sheet and report for the AGM.

How can the treasurer best carry out the job? A few dos and don'ts (also from the above mentioned publication) will give some pointers.

The treasurer's job

DO	DON'T
• Give receipts and keep a duplicate for all money received.	• Pay people out of cash you have just received.
• Enter into books an account of all money received.	• Let money owed to the group remain unpaid.
• Obtain receipts for all money paid out.	• Ask another signatory to pre-sign blank cheques for you.
• Enter into books an account of all money paid out.	• Let money pile up in a current account where it isn't earning interest.
• Bank all money received.	

It's a job that needs care and conscientiousness rather than expertise with figures, and there are lots of ways you can get help if you've never done it before.

Further advice

Remember this chapter is only a signpost. If you need more help with money matters try the following:

● Read books

A selection is listed on pages 144–5. Your local library should also be able to help. Buy any simple cheap ones that you find you need.

● Consult local sources of help

Organizations listed in the checklist on page 7 may be able to help. Some towns also have an Action Resource Centre, or a Volunteer Bureau with a professional skills register, or even a specific accountancy project.

● Get professional help

Bank managers are a traditional suggestion, but not the only possible helpers. Among or through your members you probably have access to a variety of people with relevant professional expertise.

In summary

● People first, money second.

● See money as one of the tools that makes your group work.

● Share the fund-raising jobs.

● Have fun.

● Use outside help if you want.

● Look after your money once you've got it.

Transport

Will people need to use public transport?

If possible, choose your meeting place, time and day so that people can use public transport, or where there is a car-park. Consider carefully whether you need to do anything about providing transport. In rural areas especially, it might be a crucial strand in your arrangements. Keep it as simple as possible, if you do, and use other people's vehicles if you can – community transport schemes are particularly useful and valuable. But there is more than one approach to the issue of transport, as these examples show.

★   Anne has severe rheumatoid arthritis. Each month she organizes transport for 120 members of a local arthritis group who could not get to the meeting without a lift. Transport for this group is essential. But they don't own a minibus, and Anne does the organization from her home, largely by phone.

★   Kath suffers from agoraphobia. When she first started

attending the phobics group the only way she would go was in the family car. As she got better, she tried the bus – as long as her husband drove behind so that she could get off if needed. Now she goes alone on the bus.

★ Tim suffers from depression. He is finding membership of a group of people with the same problem helpful, but it's an awful effort to get out and get there. The group's policy though is to recognize that making such an effort is part of a commitment to self help and the aims of the group. Cushioning Tim with easy transport won't help in the long term, and could make the group into a 'do-gooding-to' organization rather than the self-help group they want to be.

These three stories demonstrate the different attitudes groups will have to transport. How does your group feel about it? The following checklist may help you assess your situation.

CHECKLIST

● Where do members live? Are they so scattered that transport will be essential to get them together?

● How will the choice of meeting place help or hinder transport problems?

● How will your choice of day and time of meetings affect transport?

● Are there particular days, like market days in rural areas, when public transport is more frequent?

● Do members have a health problem which makes arranged transport essential?

● If you are a very local group is it possible for people to walk to meetings?

● Do members have their own transport?

● Will arranging transport stop people from benefiting from the results of making an effort to get there alone?

● If you don't arrange it, will they come at all?

● Is cost rather than convenience a problem?

- If you decide to provide transport, are there outside organizations that can help?

- Can members give each other lifts?

- Is it better just to assume people will make their own way?

- Can you afford to offer transport? Who will pay?

- Can you devise a system of giving people a lift home, as long as they can get to the meeting alone?

Help from outside the group

You may decide to do nothing about transport arrangements. That will simplify life considerably. If so, take particular care when choosing the meeting place, time and day, so people can either use public transport or can park.

If you decide to offer help to members, then find out whether you can get it from outside the group. One group's transport rota includes social services ambulances, volunteers' cars and a voluntary transport scheme minibus. A transport system organized by the local Lions Club in one town led to the attendance trebling at a group for people with hearing loss. Social services department ambulances and minibuses, used to take people to day centres, are made available in the evening to another group.

You could approach the following organizations:

- Social services departments (in Scotland, social work departments, in Northern Ireland, health and social services boards)

- Volunteer bureaux

- Voluntary transport schemes/car schemes

- Rotary Clubs, Lions Clubs etc.

Some members may have been introduced to the group by a social worker or health visitor. Ask if they can bring them to meetings, at least for the first few times.

Lastly, if it's cost rather than access to transport that's the problem, can you get a grant to subsidize transport costs?

One group set up to meet the needs of people being discharged from a psychiatric hospital got a subsidy through the hospital social work department. It may be possible to get a grant for travel from the local social services department.

Using members' cars

This can be a sensible, easy way to help with transport. If you're only a small group, arrangements can be made simply and the job of making sure they work can be shared out. No one minds giving the occasional lift, but if it's a regular commitment, think about sharing the cost of petrol. Insurance arrangements now allow this, as long as the car owner doesn't actually make a profit, but ask people to check that their policies cover the use of their car in this particular way.

Remember though that for many people, illness or the demands of relatives makes attendance at meetings erratic. You will need to give thought as to whether a car-sharing arrangement is reliable enough, and what will happen if people can't come – or just don't turn up.

Giving lifts is not just a practical way of getting over transport problems. It's a way of helping new members to feel welcome in a group; a chance to make friendships; an opportunity to share in a small group. But organizing a lift rota is not for every group – feel free to leave people to make their own sharing arrangements if this seems better.

Buying a minibus

Be cautious. Don't rush into this. It's a much bigger step than you might think. If you are a long-established group, providing a wide range of services, maybe even with paid staff, then it may be worthwhile. But if you are starting and running a rather less ambitious group you'd be much better off borrowing one. Minibuses may be available as part of a voluntary transport scheme, or owned by another organization and underused.

Buying your own is an attractive idea, and opens up the possibilities of outings, meetings, courses and so on immensely. But it's a seductive idea. Be realistic. Think about what it really involves:

- The initial purchase price

- Depreciation

- Running costs

- Insurance

- Tax

- Servicing

- Driving arrangements

- Availability of drivers

- Garaging

- Organizing its use

You may well decide not to buy a minibus. Think hard too about accepting the offer of one as a gift to your group. As the list above makes clear, far more is involved than just the initial outlay.

In summary

- Link your meeting arrangements to fit in with public transport

- Organize transport to meetings if essential

- Use outside help

- Don't rush into buying a minibus

Publicity

Decide whether your group needs publicity. If so, aim to arrange it seriously, spending money and time on it. Don't land one person with all the jobs – this is an opportunity for members to grow in confidence and learn new skills. There's a variety of ways of getting publicity: it's a challenge to try them out, and can be fun to do together.

Do all groups need publicity?

Does every group need publicity? You may have found some like-minded people and are meeting with them regularly, concentrating on mutual support. For you, publicity may not be needed. Or if you've decided to meet only a limited number of times, you may feel you don't want to publicize your existence. Or it may be that your problem is a very personal one – incest could be an example – in which case publicity might not be appropriate. Groups like this are probably more inward-looking to the members than outward-looking to the community: they are focusing on the needs of their members, and they've got enough of these already.

But other groups, probably a majority, will want to look outwards to the community, and will plan to include publicity in their activities. There are three reasons why publicity can be worthwhile:

- *Most groups will have a turnover in their membership.* If the group is not visible, and makes no effort to draw in new people, the numbers will fall and the group will not thrive. It may even expire before it's really started.

- *New members will join because they are attracted to the group.* Publicity about the group allows people who have a problem to know it exists, and make a decision about joining.

- *Growth in membership helps members to change their role.* As newcomers join the group, older members often feel more confident about the way they are coping. They begin to be a model for the newcomers, and have the opportunity to help others. This can often be as useful as receiving help.

What might you need publicity for?

There are several reasons why groups publicize themselves:

- To tell potential new members about a regular meeting and give them a contact person.

- To inform people about a particular meeting or event – maybe a talk or a fund-raising effort.

- To help in a campaign for change, or to fight a proposed change.

- To educate the public about a particular condition or problem.

These reasons are often related. If you seek publicity for one purpose you may in fact achieve it for another.

Is it one individual or the group that will be featured?

It's quite common for a new group to revolve round one person initially. It may be one person's desperate need that is the trigger for the group in the first place. Journalists are often more interested in a personal story than in a group, and may be more willing to give space on this basis. This may be particularly true for groups just starting. There is nothing wrong in an individual's need being at the core of things. But there are some issues which need to be considered.

- An individual can appear to be more important than the group, which is not good for the group's long-term success.

- A named person may be open to abusive telephone calls or letters, though this isn't common.

- You may find that your story is written up, or edited on tape, in a sensational way.

There are some ways round these difficulties:

- Your group can adopt a general principle of anonymity from the start.

- Change personal details or use first names or pseudonyms.

- In a feature article, several people's stories can be told, not just one.

- Use a friendly organization, or your meeting place, as an address.

- Do not give a telephone number.

- Make enquiries to help you locate sympathetic and dependable journalists.

How much publicity do you want?

'We had to take the phone off the hook in the end, there were so many calls', said one group for people with a mental health problem. Be careful – you can be too successful, and attract interest out of all proportion to the scale on which you want to operate. You could also end up attracting inappropriate enquiries if you are not very clear about your group and its membership. This can be both frustrating and painful for you and the enquirer.

Think through exactly who you are trying to attract, and how many people you can cope with. Once your numbers grow much above 15, talking problems through in a personal way in a group becomes much more difficult. If that's the main basis of your meeting, you will need to review how to cope with larger numbers. And what about the meeting place? How many people can actually fit in?

So think about the scale of publicity, the pace at which you want to grow and the methods you can use to make yourself visible.

How to get publicity

LOCAL RADIO

Local radio stations have proved invaluable to many self-help groups. Its particular advantages are:

- Many potential members are likely to be people who can't get out of the house much and so may well be listening.

- It can get a lot of detailed information across in a very short time.

- Hearing ordinary people speaking can be much more meaningful and real than written information.

There are various slots to consider – remember you'll be competing for airtime, so consider your approach. You could try to get a mention in one or more of the following ways:

- Phone-in programme
- Straight news item

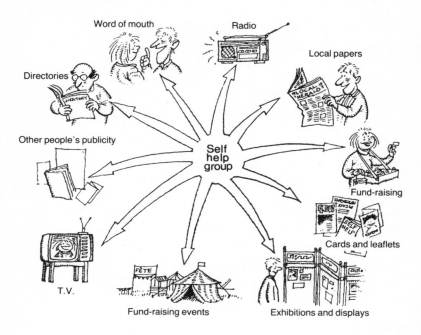

- 'What's on' announcements/diaries
- Interview with a news angle
- Specialist programme e.g. sports
- Ethnic minority programmes
- Religious spot/programme
- Public services announcement
- Making your own feature
- Special slot for self-help groups

Listen to your local radio station, before you approach it. Get the feel of the station, learn some of the presenters' names and what sort of shows they run. Find out whether they have an old or young audience.

When you contact the station, have a clear list of the main points you want to make. Just a few is better than too many. If you are planning on getting an interview, find someone in your group who can speak well.

Often the subject or the work of your group alone, though vitally important to you, is not considered interesting enough to broadcast. Try to find a news angle to your subject: the publication of a report; something controversial that has happened; a local conference; a 'national week' promoted by a national self-help organization.

If the name of your group doesn't explain clearly what it does, then add a phrase which makes it clearer.

Most people in self-help groups who go on local radio have never done it before – don't hold back for this reason.

LOCAL PAPERS

Written publicity has an advantage over radio – people can cut out the item, and think about it. This may result in them joining your group months after the article appears. Think about a local angle. Journalists on local papers will be looking for interesting events, angles and people in the neighbourhood. Think about how you can make yourself interesting. As with radio, you'll be competing for space and need to sell yourself. Consider the following ways:

- A news item
- A feature article
- Listing in a 'What's on' column
- Writing a letter to the Editor
- Advertising in the personal column (you'll have to pay)
- A photo of an event or person
- Sending them your newsletter
- Using a women's page or consumer column
- Special feature on self-help groups
- Commenting on a national report or issue

Don't forget the free papers

Many parts of the country now have free weekly papers, largely consisting of advertising, but needing material on local news and initiatives. They have proved to be very helpful for self-help groups.

How do you contact papers?

Telephone and letters are both acceptable. Personal contact with journalists is often helpful.

Established groups could consider writing a *press release*. It's not very difficult and is likely to increase your chances of getting in print. Follow these suggestions on how to do a press release:

- Use headed group notepaper and write PRESS RELEASE on it

- Include the date

- Type in double spacing

- Leave wide margins

- Type on one side of the paper only

- Give contact names, addresses and phone numbers, and times when they can be reached

- Break down your story into short paragraphs

- Make your heading interesting

- If you don't want your story printed till a certain day or time, put 'Embargoed till ——'

- Keep it short

- Don't include anything you don't want printed

You can photocopy a press release and send it to several local papers, and to radio and TV stations.

Be precise about information

If you want to put over publicity about events and meetings, be very clear about it. There are five Ws to remember:

- Who?

- What?

- Why?

- When?

- Where?

For example:

'The Alzheimer's Disease Society (a self-help group for people caring for a relative who is suffering from senile dementia) is holding a barbecue. It is being run to raise money for their new day centre, on Saturday June 26th 1986 at 7.00 p.m., at Gladehill School, Jamieson Rd, Newport. Buy your tickets (£1.50) at the gate.'

This advice on information applies to local radio too. It should be followed whether you are phoning up, writing a letter or preparing a press release.

POSTERS

Ask yourself some questions: Do you need posters? Where can you put them up? What results do they have? Be realistic: the life of a poster is probably only two weeks. People take them down, put other posters on top of them, even deface them.

If you decide to use posters, should you put them up yourselves or ask other people to distribute and put them up for you? The following organizations may be willing to do this, but you need to be quite certain the posters will be displayed. Try:

- Libraries (a central library may send posters out to branch libraries)

- Family Practitioner Committees (the central point for GPs)

- Health Authorities (Community Units will probably send posters out to health centres)

- Community Councils/CVSs (may mail out to voluntary organizations)

Think of other places relevant to your audience:

- Health food shops
- Book shops
- Social services departments
- Citizens Advice Bureaux/information centres
- Churches
- Community centres
- Hospital waiting areas

See posters as one of the ways that let people know you exist. You may not get many members directly, but posters will help build up an awareness that your group is in operation. They take time and money, but for many groups are a successful form of publicity.

CARDS AND LEAFLETS

Small cards are another way to get general, long-term publicity. If they are not too detailed they can be displayed as posters and distributed in the ways suggested above. They take up less room, are more durable and can be used in these ways too:

- Give a supply to professional workers to hand out to people they know
- Use them as hand-outs at exhibitions and events
- Send them by post to enquirers
- Put them in information racks at libraries or other public places

Leaflets will be cheaper, allow more information to be included but can't be used as substitute posters so easily.

EXHIBITIONS AND DISPLAYS

Think small until you've got the resources and membership to think big. A **full scale exhibition** is a possibility for established groups. Plan it some months in advance and be sure enough members will help to man it.

Both new and established groups can usefully consider a **display**, a small version of an exhibition. You could put it on in someone else's premises, or at someone else's event. This saves time and energy over publicity, which an exhibition will require. And it won't need members to be there beside it, as a big exhibition will. Consider:

- A building society window

- A local library

- Council for Voluntary Service/Community Council premises

- A big fund-raising event

You can probably borrow display boards – try the Health Education Unit, or a large voluntary organization, for example. Make your display simple, easy to read, colourful and eye-catching. Use big photos wherever possible. Ask other people for help in design and production.

As with posters, don't expect a sudden upsurge in your membership. Regard it as part of your public relations work – making people aware that your group and your problem exist.

FUND-RAISING EVENTS

Publicity resulting from fund-raising events may be as useful as the actual cash they produce. Photos and reports will also boost members' morale and make the hard work even more worthwhile.

Sometimes groups deliberately plan an event for maximum publicity rather than large financial benefit. Even modest efforts like Christmas card sales help people know you are around.

Taking part in someone else's fund-raising effort may be a particularly helpful way of combining the two aims. As well as cakes and plants on your stall for example, you can have some leaflets. Some groups get plastic carrier bags printed, or sell and wear T-shirts with the group's emblem on them: self-help groups can learn about selling themselves from the commercial world.

TELEVISION

Television is not a medium suitable for all groups. It's difficult to get access to, and the few minutes likely to be available may well be too short to put over a fairly complex picture of a group or an issue. If you live in an area where television has a particular local flavour, then consider it more seriously. But still bear in mind there are limitations and risks. Don't rush into television coverage, and work out whether it feels right for your group.

Groups have successfully used television in the following ways:

- Public Service Announcements/Community Service Announcements
- An in-depth programme about their work
- Focusing on an issue in a news programme
- Being part of a series on self-help groups

USING OTHER PEOPLE'S PUBLICITY

Can you think of any ways in which you can use other people's publicity? Are there any newsletters or magazines in your area that would welcome articles? Church magazines are one idea but there may be other publications in which you can get a free, or cheap slot. The principle to follow is that of taking up opportunities to get to a wider audience, without it involving you in a great deal of time and money.

Some organizations may not be able to include your group in their publication, but won't mind putting your leaflet in their envelopes – when they send newsletters to their members or subscribers, for example. Using other people's mailings can be a very helpful way of getting your leaflets or cards out with no, or low, postage costs. Your local newsagent may also let you slip a leaflet into newspapers or magazines.

DIRECTORIES

Local directories are a good way of publicizing self-help groups. One group found they got more members through an entry in a directory than in any other way. But be cautious: a directory may take up to a year to compile. Will your information still be correct when it is actually published? And even if they are updated, old directories can circulate for years. People may be very willing for their names to go in at the time, but make sure they realize the implications. They may go on getting phone calls for several years. New groups need to be particularly cautious about going in a directory, as this story demonstrates:

★ A small group of women suffering from postnatal depression were introduced to each other following a radio programme on the subject. They decided to form a group, and began to meet weekly in MIND's premises. As part of their publicity efforts, they took up an offer of a space in a directory of self-help groups. But within months they had decided to stop meeting – many of them had got better, others felt well enough to join a neighbourhood mother and toddlers group. This was great, but health visitors, seeing the group listed in the directory and welcoming its establishment, had begun to tell people about it. Several potential members turned up on the meeting night only to be disappointed and to feel rejected. The compilers of the directory are now offering space only to established groups.

Only consider having an entry in a directory once the group has been going some time. You should have:

● A regular meeting place

● A regular meeting

● At least two people who are reliable contacts

Don't put a phone number in if you can't deal with enquiries and if you do, then indicate if it's for general calls, or only for information about meetings. Give times to ring if that's possible.

You could get entries in these directories:

● A directory of voluntary or social service organizations (usually produced by a CVS, Volunteer Bureau or Community Council)

● Directories published by local papers

- Guides published by local councils
- A local self-help groups directory

Established groups, who can give a permanent group telephone number, could consider an entry in the Yellow Pages or a Thomson's Directory.

WORD OF MOUTH

Many groups have found that this was their most successful method of recruitment, and it's very cheap. If it feels right for you, encourage members to talk about the group to families and friends. But recognize too that anonymity may be more important to people. They may come to meetings without ever telling people close to them that they do so, so don't put pressure on people to be ambassadors or recruiting officers.

Do you want to review your publicity?

This checklist may help you look at your group's efforts:

CHECKLIST

- Is your publicity bringing you new members?
- Which method is most successful? Ask people how they heard of the group, when they first make contact.
- Does it all depend on one person?
- Have you got headed notepaper?
- Do you collect press cuttings? Could they be used in displays?
- Do you take photos of your activities? Could they be used in papers, reports or displays?
- Are you using all the opportunities available?
- What priority does your group want to give to publicity?

In summary

- Think through whether you need publicity.
- If so, make time and budget money for it.

- Choose the methods that feel right for your group.

- Don't be afraid to try something new.

- Evaluate how successful your publicity is.

Printing

Who needs printed material?

Put a question to yourself: is your group one that will need printed material? Most groups do, but there are some exceptions. The groups who probably won't need it are:

- Small groups, concentrating on face to face mutual support, with a stable membership and maybe meeting in homes.

- Groups meeting only over a limited time.

- Local branches of national organizations, whose parent bodies produce good literature, (but remember even then, your possible need for local identity).

Most other groups will benefit from having at least some printed material.

Can you learn from other people?

You may never have printed anything before – but lots of other small organizations have. This is an aspect of self-help group work where you can learn a lot from other small groups, not necessarily self-help ones. You can also take up offers of skilled help from outside.

You could start with a bit of investigation, not just by one person, but drawing in a number of members. Get people to bring examples of printed material from other organizations. Go – in pairs maybe – to places where there are a lot of posters, like the library, and study how effective and attractive different ones are. Would you go to *their* meeting?

Lastly, find out if there is a resource centre, or arts centre in your area which offers particular help to voluntary groups who want to produce printed material. The Council for Voluntary Service or Community Council will probably be able to advise you.

Why might you need printed material?

These could be the reasons:

- To attract new members
- To inform the public and sympathetic professionals
- To communicate with members
- To share information
- To publicize events
- To assist a campaign

These are specific aims which printing will help achieve. For new groups, there is an even more basic reason why you may need printed material: it will help you be a group. Groups are surprised to find how designing even a letterhead makes them focus hard on who they are, and what they want to do. You need a name for a start. It's not easy, but it is rewarding and it's a tangible achievement. A number of members can be involved too, indeed, if they are not, it won't be the group's material. It will appear to be that one person's only, which is not healthy for a self-help group.

What printed material might you need?

Here's a list of items self-help groups have produced. You won't need them all, of course, but it may help you decide what you need now. Come back to it again later on, when your group has been established for a while:

- Headed notepaper
- Cards
- Posters about regular meetings

- Posters giving a contact person
- Posters about special events
- Blank posters
- Badges
- Identification cards
- Copies of articles
- Summaries of talks
- Extracts from national newsletters
- Bookmarks
- Calendars
- Booklets about a particular condition
- Leaflets
- Members' newsletters
- Minutes of business meetings
- AGM minutes
- Annual reports
- Lists of useful names and addresses
- T-shirts
- Plastic carrier bags
- Calendar of group events
- Pens

What about cost?

Printing will cost money, but it need not be a huge sum. It will depend on what method you use and where you get it done. If you can learn to do it yourself, as many groups have done successfully, you will save money.

You may also be able to cut costs by drawing on outside help, getting sponsorship, applying for specific grants, getting discounts and paying cash.

Make sure the initial printing order is large enough – it costs more to go back and ask for another batch at a later date.

How can you produce printed material?

It's tempting to forget about the technicalities and print by hand. But unless you are a gifted artist, your group will look homely. It will also take enormous amounts of time. There will be occasions when hand-produced material is sensible – appeals for jumble or a small coffee morning, for example – but otherwise, unless you specially want to look homely, consider other methods: duplicating, photocopying and printing.

Duplicating

is suitable as a cheap way of reproducing medium sized quantities of A4 or A5 sized paper. (A4 is $11\frac{3}{4}$ in $\times 8\frac{1}{4}$ in, or 297 mm $\times$ 210 mm, A5 is half that size). Your text is typed on a typewriter on to a stencil, which is then run off on a duplicator, on to white or coloured paper. AGM minutes are a good example of material which could be reproduced like this.

Use of an electronic stencil cutter can allow you to produce more attractive material, though not all artwork can be done in this way. You make up your A4 sheet with typed material and simple art work, have a stencil made on the stencil cutter and then run it off on a duplicator. A cheap handout at an exhibition could be done by this method, for example.

Photocopying

is subject to legal restrictions. If you are simply copying your own minutes, there are no problems. But if you want several copies of an article, it must technically be for the purpose of private study. It's a very simple effective way of doing a small number of copies. Large machines are often of high quality and cost less. Photocopiers are very easy for anyone to operate.

Printing

is the best way to produce large quantities. You achieve high quality results and the process is much more versatile. You can include cartoons, symbols and even photos and use different colours.

Silkscreen printing is slow and laborious but is a very effective way of producing original posters and T-shirts.

Where can you get work done?

HELPFUL OUTSIDERS

The following may be able to help:

- Employers
- Social workers
- Community centres
- Churches
- Art college students
- Hospital occupational therapy departments
- Councils for Voluntary Service
- Schools

SPECIALIST RESOURCE CENTRES OR ARTS CENTRES

People living in towns may find there is a resource centre designed to help small groups produce their own printed material. A wide range of equipment is available, and usually skilled staff to help. Costs are low, and it is often an enjoyable, relaxing activity. You don't need to have any special artistic skills.

But it does take hours – so think about the time commitment first and be realistic. Also check how reliable the equipment is, look at other people's work, ask about access to the building for anyone with a handicap, opening hours and whether booking is needed. You may also need to affiliate to the centre.

LIBRARIES

Most medium sized or large libraries have photocopiers, worked by inserting coins. Their great advantage is accessibility and speed – but go equipped with change. Many of the organizations already mentioned may also be able to photocopy materials for you.

COMMERCIAL PRINTERS

While these may be more expensive, you do have advantages if you decide to use them: you save yourself time and you have more control over the process. You'll find that they prefer not to do rushed jobs, and they charge more to do a job quickly, so you will still need to plan in advance and work out a timetable. Costs vary, so shop around and get written estimates for any large job. For complicated jobs, like raffle tickets, you will have to go to a printer.

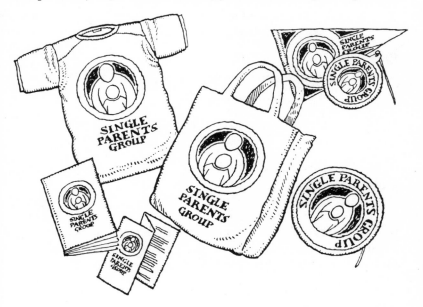

CHECKLIST

- Can you produce your publicity material yourselves?

- Are there any helpful outsiders who can assist?

- How quickly do you need to produce it?

- What will it cost?

- How can you pay for it?

- Can you adopt a group symbol, and use it on all your publicity material?

- Can you use cartoons?

- Can you adopt a special group colour and use it systematically?

- Can people with poor sight read what you produce?

- Can you draw in members with special talents or time?

- Do you need to revise old publicity material?

- How can you make producing it fun rather than a chore?

- Can producing printed material together help your members grow in skills and confidence?

In summary

- Produce simple attractive publicity material

- Involve members in its production

- Use sources of help from outside

Communication

Rooms, money, printing and so on: these are practical issues that self-help groups have to tackle. Communication is less easy to identify, but equally important to a group's success.

Why is communication important?

- It improves contact between people in groups.

- It allows members to understand what is going on.

- It gives people more opportunity to join in.

Communication takes different forms in self-help groups.

TALKING

- Talking in the group or in one-to-one discussions.

- Talking on the telephone.
- Using tapes and videos.

WRITING

- Publicity material, group newsletters, distribution of minutes.
- Personal letters to individual members.
- A scrapbook or group diary.
- Writing on a blackboard or flipchart.
- Using notice boards.

EXCHANGING FEELINGS

- Tears
- Smiles and laughter
- Silence
- Handshakes and hugs.

How good is communication in your group?

CHECKLIST

- How many members do you know by name?
- How many names do new members know?
- How do people find out about special activities?
- How do new members find out about earlier decisions made by the group?
- If someone has a new idea, how do they put it forward?
- How, if at all, do members communicate outside meetings?
- How do new members find out about contact outside meetings?
- Is there an informal part to your meeting for one-to-one chat?

- Does the room where you meet help or hinder communication?

- Is there time in your meetings to discuss arrangements and future plans?

- Do people trust each other?

- Are discussions confidential?

- Does your group's problem restrict communication at all?

What specially affects communication in self-help groups?

Size makes a lot of difference. A group with a membership of 15 or less will be rather different to that of over 15. Really big numbers bring other challenges.

Turnover of membership will affect how much effort you need to put into communication. A stable group may not need to explain matters so much, but runs the risk of making newcomers feel left out. It's wise to assume you'll have some turnover, so plan communication to meet the needs of new members.

The problem facing members will influence the way you communicate. In particular, if people have any hearing loss, visual handicap or problems with speech, you'll need to think through together how best to tackle the situation.

The structure of the group, and of the meetings, will affect how well you communicate and what methods you use. Groups who meet infrequently, for example, may put more emphasis on telephone links and newsletters. Groups who form a committee will need to consider how the committee communicates with the rest of the group.

A feeling of equality among members makes communication easier. If certain people dominate discussions, new members or people uncertain of themselves will hesitate to join in. Communication will be easier in groups where everyone feels they have something to contribute, and are encouraged to do so.

How might you increase communication between old and new members?

Groups have found that they are more effective if there are ways of old and new members sharing their experience. You can't leave this to chance: groups need to plan how this can be achieved in their particular setting.

Think whether any of these methods could work in your group:

- Having a set time in meetings when older members can tell their story.

- Giving space in newsletters for people to write about their experiences.

- Welcoming new members at the door.

- Offering a one-to-one link outside the group.

- Sharing transport to and from meetings.

- Running short courses on listening and befriending.

- Building in time for social contact at meetings and events.

- Having a committee member with special responsibility for introducing new members.

In summary

- Question how well you communicate.

- Think what affects communication in your group.

- Make sure there is communication between old and new members.

Relationships

Relationships with each other

How your group is run is important. It needs to be formal enough to be well organized, but friendly enough to make new members feel welcome and involved. Getting the right balance between the two isn't easy, but it can be done.

Do self-help groups need a structure?

It may be tempting to drift along without any system of organizing yourselves, but don't succumb to temptation. Groups do need some sort of structure – a framework is needed so that:

- Decisions are taken

- No one person dominates the group

- The group has stability and continuity

- New members understand what is going on

- New ideas can be introduced

It need not be complicated. Keep your structure simple. You can always add to a simple structure but it is much more difficult to take away from one which is over elaborate.

What sort of structure is suitable?

There is no one way of organizing a self-help group, and your group will need to make its own decisions. One way of approaching it is like other organizations: to elect a committee, with a chairperson, secretary and treasurer. They hold office until the next

Annual General Meeting, when they may well get re-elected. They hold separate committee meetings and report back to the members.

But just because this works for other organizations is it the best way to run a self-help group? This traditional structure may in fact be too formal and prevent people from taking part. While it may suit some groups, don't assume it's automatically right for you. These following stories show there are other ways of doing it.

★ *Depressives Anonymous* (DA), like a number of anonymous groups, has learnt a lot from AA. One particular local branch meets weekly – the meetings are the main source of support – and has an attendance of 8–12. The group has evolved a pattern which is followed at each meeting, so anyone can act as chairperson. This job is shared around among most members. There is however a named treasurer who holds the job for a year and he or she looks after the small amount of money that is involved. If there is some special piece of business to discuss – a change of meeting room for example – it's done in the whole group, convening a special meeting if necessary.

★ *Toc M* stands for Two O'clock Mondays – when a group of physically handicapped people, all over 60, meet together in a member's house. They have kept their numbers small so that they can continue to meet in this way. The group emerged from several members being introduced to each other by an occupational therapist – but she just acts as back-up. The group has a chairperson, treasurer and secretary who take on the usual jobs – but special outings and visits are often organized by other members. They deal with most of the business in their ordinary meetings.

★ A local *Phobics* Group was set up from the beginning with a 'Trustees' Committee' and a formal constitution. The committee had responsibility for finance and for ensuring the group operated within the constitution. The group had difficulties. Members saw the need for more involvement in decision making and tasks by the whole group. They decided they needed better communication; creation of time and space for discussion; and flexibility over the contribution of each group member. They've now devised ways of achieving these while retaining the original framework.

What should you take into account?

When considering what sort of organization is right for you, it's helpful to think about a number of things. The following checklist may help.

CHECKLIST

- How big is your group now?

- How large might it become?

- Are you going to restrict numbers?

- Do you live in the town or country? Is lack of transport going to affect the way you organize the group?

- Are any professionals involved in the group? What is their role?

- Do you have, or want, a formal constitution?

- Are you a branch of a national organization? Do they insist on certain rules for the way you run?

- Are you concentrating on mutual support, or running a variety of activities?

- How much money does your group have? How much might it have in the future?

- How can you share the jobs out?

- Can you rotate positions of responsibility?

- How could your structure encourage older members to stay on in the group?

- Do you receive grants from outside bodies?

- Do they require evidence of the way you are organized? (e.g. set of rules; constitution, names of officers)

- Do people in your group have strong personalities?

- Do members have personal problems which make taking on responsibility difficult?

- Can you visit any other local self-help groups and learn from them?

Do you need a leader?

The group will need to be led, but it doesn't necessarily need one leader. If you are a large group, and decide to adopt a formal committee model, you will probably share the jobs of leadership out in a traditional way: chairperson, secretary, treasurer.

Some groups add other jobs to this list. They might have some of the following: vice chairperson; minutes secretary; social secretary; librarian; publicity officer. Sharing the jobs in this way is a good idea in principle, but don't take it so far that it becomes unworkable.

Smaller groups, often using the experience of AA, may decide not to have a leader, except one person as secretary/treasurer. Their job might be to look after the small amount of money, make sure the room is booked and coffee available and take care of the literature. The rest of the job of leading the group is done by the other members.

A third way of leading the group could be one adopted by some small 'therapeutic' groups. These are self-help groups which are nearer in spirit to groups run by professional workers. They may well limit their membership – what is called being a 'closed group' – and appoint a person as a leader.

Make sure your group gets led rather than drifts. But choose the way it is led to suit you and your needs, and avoid domination by any one individual.

Successful organization

The following suggestions may help you in your search for the way your group can best be organized and led.

- Choose a structure which allows most members to join in.

- Encourage new members to take on jobs.

- Consider limiting the time for which anyone can hold a position of leadership.

- Keep simple records, so that jobs can be passed on without too much difficulty.

- Don't let discussions about organization take over the whole meeting.

- Encourage some older members to stay on and take on responsibilities, but don't let them dominate the group forever.

- Avoid the development of cosy 'cliques'.

Don't be boring!

What difficulties might leaders face?

However you organize your group, people in any position of leadership will face difficulties. This guide doesn't try to tell you how to solve these, but it may help to know some of the situations that self-help groups have had to face. Just knowing that you are not the only one tackling the issue may help. Here are some examples of difficulties that have arisen in groups:

● Inertia among members

● People who talk too much

● Domination by a few people with one interest

● Disruptive behaviour

● Group leaders being unable to share their own problems

As the group goes on, some of these difficulties may well resolve themselves. Leadership is not easy, but you can learn from experience. Don't be discouraged too soon – see it as a challenge, not an insoluble problem.

In summary

● Adopt some structure in your group

● Go for simplicity

● A group needs leadership, but not necessarily one leader

Relationships with national organizations

Self-help groups are essentially local bodies. Face to face contact or local phone calls will be the way most people take part in them. If there is a national link-up, and many groups have found this helpful, probably only a minority of members will be involved.

There are two types of national organization that you might have contact with. The first are *general organizations*, such as those listed on pages 147–8. They may well produce useful publications, provide advice, or organize conferences. On the whole – especially if you are new – they are several steps removed from your local concern, and you may never need to contact them.

The organization that you are more likely to have a relationship with is a *national self-help organization*, which concerns itself with the same issue as your group, but on a national scale.

National self-help organizations vary a great deal – in size, resources, aims and structure. They may regard themselves as having close links with professional care and may even be dominated by professional workers. Or they may be fiercely independent, probably highly critical of professional services, operating as a pressure group or advocating alternative care.

The following five types of relationship between national bodies and local self-help groups are all possible.

NO NATIONAL ORGANIZATION EXISTS

You've no choice here. If you set a group up, it's simply a local group. If you need support, or signposts to information and help, you'll have to look to local organizations for back-up. There may be other local groups tackling the same problem in other parts of the country, but you'll be lucky if you find them. On the other hand, you have a free hand in what you try to do and you can give all your time to developing your local work.

STARTING LOCAL, AFFILIATING NATIONALLY LATER

A number of self-help groups have happily started as a local body. They may not have known that a national organization existed or decided to delay a decision on whether to join till they found their feet. If you're like this, you may find the national body requires you to make some changes in your group and you may need to give them some money. There are many benefits in starting this way, enabling you to take one step at a time.

You will be able to concentrate on establishing your local group rather than perhaps feeling obliged to raise funds or join in national meetings all the time. And once you do affiliate you will be strong enough to decide yourselves how active a part you would like to play nationally and what sort of back-up you need from the national organization.

STARTING LOCAL, STAYING LOCAL

Others have started the same way but decided to stay as an independent local body. There are also examples of groups who affiliate for a time, and then withdraw from their parent national body. There is no compulsion to have a formal relationship – and indeed as the list of disadvantages on page 83 shows, there can be benefits in being totally local and independent. It depends a lot on what you are trying to do, and your priorities.

Perhaps the happiest compromise form of relationship is where local groups remain autonomous, but have the opportunity to use a national body. They may draw on it for information and advice, or use it as a means of linking up with other local groups. This probably doesn't happen very often.

NATIONAL ORGANIZATION INITIATES LOCAL GROUP

Like the first possibility, there is no element of choice here. You will be starting as a local branch of a national body, and will have to include the requirements of your parent organization in your aims and structures. This will mean less flexibility but brings advantages. Remember though that groups have found that relationships between national bodies and local branches are not wholly easy. It will be particularly important to make space in your local meetings for sharing personal problems – it's all too easy for discussions about branch rules and donations to head office to crowd out mutual support.

OPERATING LOCALLY, BUT FINDING YOURSELF NATIONAL

This is an uninvited and sometimes difficult situation. You may be a pioneer in your field. Though your aims are to set up a local group, and the local group begins and operates well, you find yourself being regarded as a national resource. 'Can you help us get going?' 'Will you visit us?' 'Can we visit you?' 'How do I become a registered charity?' There have been examples of people being overwhelmed with requests like this. If it happens to you, you'll need to work out strategies for dealing with them. Make your own local group and your personal needs take first place. You may consider setting up a national organization is the answer, but be aware that this too is a major and time-consuming task.

More difficult may be personal requests for help from people in trouble who live many miles way. Be supportive but realistic about your limits, and don't hesitate to remind them of the Samaritans (listed under S in telephone directories).

You may feel you are rejecting people. Don't think of it as rejection, think of it as setting boundaries to what you and your group feel able to do well and happily.

If you find yourself catapulted into such a situation, be wary of the media. There have been bad examples of people's personal stories being overdramatized and overpublicized, bringing distress rather than progress. The press can be enormously helpful in the development of national organizations and issues – but be careful.

Affiliation to a national organization or not?

Affiliation to a national body and independence both bring advantages and disadvantages. Whichever you opt for, the list on page 83 may help you perceive the strengths and weaknesses.

RELATIONSHIPS CAN BE DIFFICULT

Groups have found that relationships between local branches and national self-help organizations are not always easy. There may well be a conflict of interest. For example, local groups may be concerned with mutual support and information; national bodies may focus on fund-raising, research and co-operative relationships with professionals.

There may too be unrealistic expectations. Groups may feel they don't get help and support and national bodies may set unrealistic targets for group activities and fund-raising. Control is another

POSSIBLE ADVANTAGES

An umbrella to shelter under.

Practical back-up:
speakers, literature,
publicity material.

Personal support from people
with knowledge of your
problem.

Links with other similar local
groups.

Provision of address lists of
national members.

Easy registration as a charity.

Opportunities to campaign on
national issues.

Help with setting up projects.

Rescue at times of crisis.

Training and handbooks.

Welfare services for members.

Credibility.

Opportunities to contribute to
research.

International links.

Links with other voluntary
and statutory bodies.

POSSIBLE DISADVANTAGES

Wish for control over local
groups.

Tension over fund-raising by
local branches for national
body.

Inflexibility and insistence on
a particular structure.

Conflict over aims and
priorities.

Expectations of support
unfulfilled.

High cost of attending national
meetings and conferences.

Expectation of attendance at
national meetings conflicts
with local needs.

Sheer distance and
remoteness.

South of England base of most
national self-help
organizations.

Tension over campaigning.

Too close an association
between national body,
professionals and government.

National organization stagnant
while local group progressive.

Insistence on membership
subscriptions going wholly or
in part to national body.

difficult issue. To what extent, should and can national bodies control local self-help groups? On the more positive side, national organizations which manage to get frequent friendly contact between local branches and themselves, find relationships work well and groups appreciate the link.

It is easy for national bodies of any sort to get stagnant. Involvement by local group members, as committee members or regional representatives can prevent this happening. They are in an ideal situation to put forward new ideas and to act as a link with the membership. If groups remain parochial, national bodies will not receive the stimulus that will come from their involvement.

On a personal level too this can be productive. People who move on from purely local self-help work to participate on national committees can find it exciting and fulfilling.

Fundamentally remember that your group is local, meeting local people's needs in a particular area. When you are starting, especially, this will need to be your priority.

In summary

- Be realistic about the complexity of the relationship between local and national organizations.

- Consider carefully the strengths and disadvantages that arise from affiliation.

- Go for co-operation, not conflict, and make your own decision.

Relationships with local professional workers

Local professional workers are an important set of people. What might your relationship be with them? This chapter is about people working in a paid, professional way in the caring services. They are likely to be in the field of health and social services or perhaps education. They will mostly be employed by a statutory body, that is, the Health Authority, a Regional, County or District Council or a Family Practitioner Committee. Some may be employed to do a professional job in one of the big voluntary organizations, like the NSPCC.

While their jobs vary enormously, they will nearly all have had several years training, and often many years' experience. Their fairly precise job description is unlikely to include support to self-help groups – any work they do with you will be because they interpret their job in that way, or, sometimes, do it in their own time.

There is often a certain amount of status attached to professional jobs. Some professionals still see themselves as superior to the people who are being helped. This is changing, but as you may know from your own experience, it still happens.

Self-help groups might work with the following professionals. Though, of course, not all groups will link with all of them.

- Doctors (consultants and their team, and GPs)
- Social workers (in hospitals and in area or patch teams)
- Health visitors (often now attached to GP practices)
- Physiotherapists
- Occupational therapists
- Dieticians
- Hospital administrators
- Nurses in hospitals
- District nurses and midwives
- Psychologists
- Counsellors
- Lecturers
- Health education officers
- Probation officers

What are they likely to know about self-help groups?

You can probably expect that most local professional workers will
have a positive, welcoming attitude to self-help groups. They will
know about some already, but may well get them confused with
more traditional voluntary organizations like the Red Cross or the
Samaritans. They are unlikely to have had much experience of
working closely with individual groups.

Professional training is unlikely to have equipped these people with
knowledge about self-help groups, or allowed them to think
through their attitudes to you. And in some cases training and
personality may lead them to believe that their relationship should
be one of control and leadership, though this is changing.

Professional workers might have the following expectations of you;
most will probably have a combination of these attitudes.

POSITIVE ATTITUDES

- They will welcome people
  who are doing things for
  themselves.

- They will recognize that
  members know what it's
  like to cope.

- They'll acknowledge that
  professionals don't have
  the same insight.

- They will welcome the
  opportunity groups give
  to their members to be
  helpful to other people.

- They will recognize that
  they don't have time for
  everything themselves.

NEGATIVE ATTITUDES

- Anxiety that groups will
  make people worse, not
  better.

- Fear that groups will
  hand out medical advice.

- Fear that professionals
  might be replaced if self
  help proves successful.

- Simple ignorance about
  self-help groups.

- Worries that self-help
  groups will criticize
  professionals.

- Lack of trust that 'clients'
  and 'patients' can take
  responsibility.

Even workers with very positive attitudes may be baffled by the
problem of actually finding self-help groups. And when they have

located them, they may be unaware of the way groups can quickly change or disband. They will have more experience with and probably feel more comfortable about working with organizations, both statutory and voluntary, who are a bit more predictable. Self-help groups may baffle them!

What do you think about professional workers?

Your attitudes may be coloured by your own personal experience and the particular professionals you have met. You may have had no help, or a great deal of help. Reflect on your own experience.

Some people may already have been a member of a group brought together by professional workers as a mutual support group – but led by the professionals. This may have been helpful, but it's not quite the same as a self-help group. Your experience there may influence your attitude to groups and professionals, especially to taking responsibility for the group. It may have led you to want to take the lead yourself, or to you finding it easier to sit back and let other people do the jobs.

Your group may be highly critical of professionals. Professional care may well have resulted in no help for your problem, or it may not have existed at all. The stimulus for your group may have come from despair and desperation.

Lastly – and this is probably the most common attitude – you may have appreciated the care, concern and practical help you've had, but think it's not enough. You're now looking to a self-help group for a different sort of help and support. You see it as complementary to professional care.

Does your group want to co-operate?

No one says that you must: it's your choice. In some circumstances groups may operate in a very self-contained way, with little contact with professional workers:

- If you have started as a real alternative to professional care.

- If you are making campaigning for change your first priority.

- If you are afraid of being taken over by professional workers.

- If you do not know any professionals to whom you might relate comfortably.

But think positively about fostering relationships. Good contacts and understanding have proved for many groups to be significant in contributing to their success. Important practical help for the group can result and a relationship of mutual education and partnership can evolve. Most groups will benefit from starting from a point of seeking co-operation and back-up.

However, you also need to think through the basis for any partnership. Who is in control?

What should be the basis for your relationship?

Perhaps it's useful to think back to the points that were raised about who should be members of a self-help group. If you decide that it's only going to be people experiencing the problem, or their families, who are members, then it becomes clear that professional workers are not members. However sympathetic and helpful, they are outsiders.

Both you, and the professionals, need to be aware of this status. It's not a criticism, or a second-class label. But it does clarify that the group, made up of members, is the means by which decisions are taken and priorities are set. Professionals should not tell you what to do.

But you can helpfully see professionals as supporters. Your relationship is likely to be more fruitful if you make it clear that you welcome support and back-up – on your terms – and that you want to work out ways in which you can work together.

You should not expect professional workers to 'refer' people to you. It is not the same as them referring patients for, say, physiotherapy or dietary advice to fellow professionals. You want their help with publicity but the relationship is not one of referral. Referral loses sight of the fact that people must themselves be motivated to take part in a self-help group – not go just because their social worker 'thinks it would do them good'. It implies that a

self-help group is a predictable, organized and continuing service.
And it offers temptation to the odd professional who can't think
what to do with a client they are having no success with! Instead,
think in terms of professional workers telling people that a group
exists, and how to find it.

How do you find supportive professionals?

Personal contact is probably the best way. It's very likely that
within your group you know of people that you could approach.
And if you need to find other professional workers, use your first
contact as a link in the chain. For example, a sympathetic social
worker may well be able to suggest a doctor to come and give a talk
– and may make an initial approach for you. A health visitor may
devise a method with you for getting a GP to tell his or her patients
that your group has started.

If this fails, try your local Community Health Council. They are
often very informed about the way organizations work and about
individual personalities and will act as a helpful signpost. Or for
contacting professionals outside the health service, try the CVS,
Community Council or Volunteer Bureau. Other people in the
community such as the clergy may well provide an introduction
too.

Positive ways of relating to professional workers

PUBLICITY/NEW MEMBERS

Professional workers can't usually tell you about possible members
because of the need for confidentiality. But they can tell individual
potential members about you. And they can put up publicity
material in places like waiting rooms. You can help by producing
small cards, leaflets and posters and asking them to use and display
them. If details of your group change, you'll need to replace them –
not an easy task.

Once they've got to know you, professionals can also act as a useful
link between your group and people who might join it. People

sometimes want to discuss the idea with a friendly neutral person before they join a group. You can help by keeping key professionals in touch. Ways in which you can do this include sending them newsletters and having occasional open evenings as well as some of the ways listed below. Or once you are established, you may decide to put on a display, maybe with other self-help groups, it could be at a special event at a hospital for example. 'We don't need to be converted, but we do need to be reminded of where you are and what you do' said a health visitor.

PRACTICAL HELP

You may have picked up some ideas from earlier sections on the various forms of practical help that groups have got from professional workers. These include:

- Free meeting rooms (but remember the disadvantages)
- Transport
- Secretarial help
- A place for a fund-raising event
- Printing

You may find it worthwhile getting to know the office staff in social work departments and so forth as well as the social workers. Some groups have benefited not only from their typing, but from help at fund-raising events and with transport.

CONTACT ADDRESS

There are sometimes disadvantages in giving a member's address and telephone number as the contact for the group. Some groups have benefited, in the early days especially, by being able to give a particular ward, or social work department as a contact point. It is important to be sure this will not prevent potential members enquiring. If it's an 'alternative' group you are setting up, then this may not be appropriate. It will probably only apply in a minority of cases.

SPEAKERS

It's quite common for groups to be searching for speakers on aspects of their condition, or ways in which they can cope with it better. Inviting a knowledgeable professional worker is a good way, not only to get information, but to build up a relationship with them. And they have the chance to look at you. You can help by giving them plenty of notice and a choice of dates; inviting them to come to only part of the meeting, if that's easier; being clear about the length and focus of their talk; and offering to pay travel expenses. When they come, make a special effort to make it an enjoyable and constructive evening. This could be the trigger to a future productive relationship.

MONEY

Places like hospital social work departments often have a small amount in their budget which they can use to help new groups. This may be a quick, informal way to get those early sums which mean such a lot. Be specific about what you need the money for, and keep the request small. Later, a professional worker may well be very helpful in helping you apply for larger sums of money, both in filling in forms and adding a letter of support.

PROJECTS

Some groups decide to move on from giving mutual support through talking, to setting up services and starting projects. Help from outsiders can be invaluable here, especially in assessing need and setting realistic targets. And practical back-up – transport for a weekly club, for example – may make an idea a reality.

It may be worth setting up a special small planning group to which friendly professionals are invited. Their expertise could save you from making mistakes. It is also a good way to involve them in the group for a limited time. While it is rarely appropriate for professionals to be at all committee or group meetings, certainly not as full members, co-option on to a project planning group can be good for everyone.

GENERAL SUPPORT

'It's important for people to do things for themselves' said a perceptive social worker. But it can be a lonely business for the key people starting and running a self-help group. Even if tasks are shared out, in reality it often happens that most of them go to a few leading members. A sensitive professional, who is aware that they must not take over the group, can be invaluable as back-up support to key members. This may be provided through attendance at some meetings, but also through personal contacts and phone calls. A professional's perception of the group from a friendly but outsider's stance may help you to see more clearly how to approach issues, set priorities and to deal with difficult personal relationships. 'She's there when you need her', was a warm tribute to a hospital social worker from one group.

This type of help depends very much on confidence and friendship between the group and the professional concerned, and it's often not simple for the professional to give. But it can be invaluable at the beginning; when numbers drop; and at times of change or crisis. Perhaps it works best when it grows out of doing some practical work together.

STUDENT ATTACHMENTS

Some groups have had a student linked with them for a time. If the attitude of the student is one of enabling rather than leading, then this can be a fruitful partnership, providing the terms of the attachment are worked out well together in advance. Students, particularly from social work courses, have successfully:

- Helped new groups get going

- Undertaken surveys of members' needs

- Reviewed the work of the group with its members

- Helped to launch new projects

Not only has the group benefited, but students learn an enormous amount about self-help groups. 'I'm going back to my job with so much useful knowledge that I'll put into practice' said one. In the long term this can only be helpful to groups.

If you would like to investigate this further, contact your nearest university or polytechnic. Find out if there is a course for social workers, and which tutor is responsible for arranging placements. These are often planned six months ahead, so allow time. There may be other relevant courses which also require students to do some practical work.

A MEANS FOR INCREASED INDIVIDUAL ADVICE AND BENEFITS

Many self-help groups provide information and advice for their members, particularly on welfare benefits and services. Some become immensely knowledgeable. But some problems may still stump you, and if you are new you won't have built up an information service.

Groups have successfully drawn on professionals in two ways. Individual problems can often be quickly solved by a phone call from the group to a friendly professional. And the group's knowledge about what they can benefit from can increase greatly if you organize occasional talks.

★   'I didn't realize I was entitled to attendance allowance till I heard John speak at the group' said Sylvia. A counsellor supporting a group of parents of handicapped children had been able to arrange for a welfare benefits adviser to give a talk. The group encouraged Sylvia to apply – people can find it difficult to apply for benefits that they are entitled to – and the counsellor helped her fill in the application. Sylvia now has her attendance allowance.

GIVING YOUR GROUP CREDIBILITY

Self-help groups flourish in an atmosphere of trust and support. They can die if there is an atmosphere of disapproval and criticism. Professional workers can contribute to creating a supportive atmosphere. Those who have got to know groups can help them immensely by passing information to their colleagues, spreading information and giving the opportunity for criticism and doubts to be debated. Ask supportive professionals to bridge the gap to their fellow workers.

Can you help professionals?

These topics have largely concentrated on help from professionals to you. Are there any ways in which you can be helpful to them? Groups have successfully co-operated as follows:

- Providing clear information about the group (contact person, who can join, etc.)

- Giving talks (to students, to group practice meetings, to social workers' lunch clubs)

- Co-operating with research

- Giving feedback on services

- Suggesting new services

- Helping people to understand the impact of a problem on a patient and their family

- Acting as a link between people in need of professional help and the statutory services

- Fund-raising for equipment

- Co-writing booklets on how to cope with a particular illness

Even one of these ways will help improve relationships and make it one of mutual education and support. Perhaps this is the way to see the overall relationship.

Is it an easy relationship?

It all depends. It can be one of mutual exchange and learning with everyone appreciating the improvements and opportunities that have been created. But it can also be one of friction, lack of understanding and even battles. Problems can arise from the self-help group as much as from the professional.

All friendships and support take time to evolve. Be realistic about this, take it steadily and be prepared to remake contact as people change jobs. Be confident about your ability to start and run a self-help group but remember professional workers may not see it in the same light to begin with. Concentrate on small steps of success and increased understanding between you, rather than trying to take on the whole professional world.

In summary

Be self-contained if really necessary, but your group is likely to benefit from evolving good relationships with professional workers. They won't all find it easy, but will probably be positive and supportive. They may give you a lot of practical help, and you can help them.

Drawing on local sources of help

There are other local sources of help that you could consider. Many of them have already been mentioned – this chapter summarizes them and may jog your memory.

First, remember three important points:

● You and your fellow members should decide on the member-ship, aims and priorities of your group yourselves, and how it should be run.

● Share the jobs out as far as possible, while being realistic about the fact that some people will join in more than others.

● Co-operation with local professional workers can lead to mutual education and support.

Bear these in mind when looking at the question of other local sources of help.

Is it worth looking for support?

Some small groups, who have decided to be inward-looking rather than outward-looking, may not feel the need to develop other links or a network of support. That's fine – it may be the best way for you to run.

For many groups though, it may be profitable to look for back-up and help from outside. Groups have found that there are three particular reasons why this could be so:

HANDICAPPING CONDITIONS HANDICAP THE GROUP TOO

The problem which is common to members of a group may handicap the group as well as the individuals in it. Drawing on outside help may make your group more effective. It may release your energy and time for the things you are particularly good at. How does your problem affect the group? It could be a physical or mental illness for example which makes communication, travel or regular attendance difficult. Members may be caring for dependent relatives. Outside back-up and resources could help sort out these issues, which are very common in self-help groups.

THE MORE YOU HAVE, THE MORE YOU CAN DO

Groups are often on a spiral. Those with few members and few resources may spiral, maybe rather sadly downwards while those with even a few active members seem to be able to generate resources, increase membership and so spread the load as they spiral upwards. There is a chain of benefit.

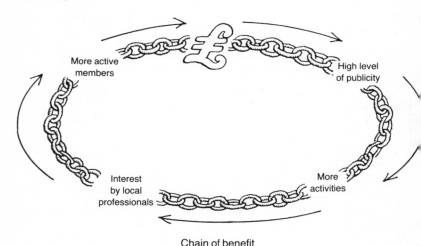

Chain of benefit

SELF-HELP GROUPS FLOURISH IN AN ATMOSPHERE OF APPROVAL

This goodwill does not only have to come from professional workers. A feeling that the whole community welcomes and admires your efforts can really spur you on. Back-up, even in a very modest way, is a way that they can put their approval into practice. Groups based on a problem surrounded by a lot of stigma or misunderstanding, even prejudice, may find it more difficult to start and to keep going. Asking for support from the local community may well break down barriers and give you more credibility.

What sort of help might you get?

- Practical help – money, rooms, secretarial services and so on.

- Publicity for members, campaigns, spreading information.

- Support for key officers in particular (as suggested from professional workers).

- Specialized information to supplement your own information service.

When can help be particularly helpful?

There are three particular times when outside help is especially valuable – whether it comes from professional workers or local organizations.

WHEN YOU ARE STARTING

If you've read this far, you'll have realized that it's not an easy job to start a self-help group. Many have foundered through not seeking and accepting back-up at this stage.

AT TIMES OF CHANGE

Stable groups may not need much outside help. But groups who change in size, meeting place and so forth may benefit from it. New officers of groups are likely to welcome general support, and a group which changes direction may want some outside guidance. Those which change from being totally voluntarily run to having a paid member of staff will be particularly wise to seek outside advice. This has proved to be a specially difficult, though challenging time.

AT TIMES OF CRISIS

This is more difficult if the crisis is internal: personality conflicts, intrusion of religion or politics, say. You may be the only people who can resolve it, painful though it may be to confront each other. But a sensitive outsider may be useful as a sounding board and source of calm, uninvolved comment. Practical crises, like losing a meeting room or transport arrangements breaking down, could well benefit from help from outside the group.

From whom might you get help?

As the previous chapter has shown, the best source may be local professional workers. But for a number of reasons, they may not be appropriate, or you may not need the type of help they can give. The chart on page 99 suggests a wide variety of local organizations that may exist in your area, and it indicates the sort of help that they might offer, or you might ask for.

Sympathetic individuals

Some organizations and resources may be easily available in your area, others may not. If you do find relevant local organizations, remember that the individuals within them are just as important as the aims and outlook of the agency. To paint an ideal picture, you'll probably get most help from sympathetic people who also:

- Have relevant knowledge and insight

- Have personal strength

- Understand how organizations start and develop

- Want to see you succeed, not take the limelight themselves

	POSSIBLE HELP			
Source of help	Practical back-up	Publicity	General support	Specialized information
Action Resource Centre	★			★
Adult Education Centre	★	★		
Advice Centre		★		★
Arts Centre	★	★		
Church	★	★	★	
Citizens' Advice Bureau		★		★
Community Centre	★	★		
Community Council	★	★	★	
Community Health Council	★	★	★	★
Community Relations Council	★	★	★	★
Community workers	★		★	
Counselling Centre	★		★	★
Council for Voluntary Service	★	★	★	★
DHSS				★
DIAL (Disablement Information Advice Line)				★
Family Centre	★		★	
Health Centre	★	★		
Leisure Centre	★	★		
Library	★	★		★
MIND	★	★	★	★
Newspapers	★	★		
Parish Council	★	★		
Pubs	★			
Radio Station	★	★		
Resource Centre	★	★		
Rotary Clubs etc.	★			
Rural Community Council	★	★	★	
Self-Help Support Scheme	★	★	★	★
Shops	★	★		
Village halls and colleges	★	★		
Voluntary Service organizers	★	★	★	
Volunteer Bureau	★	★	★	

You'll be lucky if you find someone like this! And you may not of course find support in the first agency you contact. Don't be disappointed if it doesn't work out – try some more. Think through your approach before making your initial contact. It will be helpful to be clear about your needs and to take or send information about your group.

When a good relationship does evolve, remember it's not just the specific bit of help that is important. Linking up with the local community and getting its support implies recognition of your group. And it breaks down barriers of stigma and prejudice.

In summary

Outward-looking groups can benefit from back-up from local organizations, especially when beginning and at times of change and crisis.

Contacts with other local self-help groups

It's perhaps surprising that self-help groups based on very different problems have much in common. But people who have had the chance to share knowledge and difficulties enthuse about the pleasure they get from meeting each other. 'It makes you feel you're not alone' said Jan, after a discussion evening on the relationships groups have with professional workers. She discovered that her group was not the only one finding them difficult. Individual members of a specific self-help group find relief in discovering they are not the only one with a problem. Jan and her group got support and practical ideas in a similar way from other self-help groups.

This feeling of understanding comes too because most people in groups are experiencing very deep personal problems. They often seem to identify with each other because of this. 'You understand, you're in the groups.' Barbara was sharing a personal problem about the death of her child. She'd met some members of self-help groups, other than her own, at a conference, and found herself able to talk freely in their company. Though their personal problems were very different, she knew instinctively that as fellow self-helpers they would understand.

All groups or some groups?

If you belong to a national organization, you may well have the opportunity to meet similar groups in other towns. This can be immensely useful, but travel, time and money all limit the frequency of meetings, and areas vary so much that groups don't always identify with each other.

People have found that there is some value stemming from contact between self-help groups in the same area. But should this be with all groups or just a few?

Sometimes it's very useful for there to be contact – and maybe action – between all, or most of, the groups who work in the same area. But this isn't the only approach. You may benefit from smaller networks:

- Groups who are facing a very similar problem, being the parent of a handicapped child for example, can find links with other groups valuable.

- Groups which are similar in their organization, perhaps the 'anonymous' groups, may feel a common identity and want to learn from each other.

- Groups who meet in the same building – a health centre maybe – could find it helpful to get together occasionally.

There is room for plenty of flexibility.

Simple ways of having contact

You need to be realistic about how much time you can spare for joint activities. The following examples are some very simple ways of having contact, which don't need much time or money and which you can arrange yourself.

VISITING EACH OTHER

A few people from one group can usually easily arrange to go to another group's meeting. Some, especially those based on anonymity, may prefer this to be at an 'open meeting', but others don't mind visitors sitting in on any meeting. It's best to phone first.

★　Liz was seeking help with her eating problems by starting a new group but neither local group concerned with eating – Anorexic Aid and Overeaters Anonymous – focused on her needs. She sensibly used her visits to their meetings to help her find out more about how different self-help groups function, and to establish links with similar groups.

Liz's visits were to other similar groups. But if you actually want to see how self-help groups organize themselves, how they tackle practical problems or relate to professional workers, you could actually go to any self-help group.

JOINT SPONSORSHIP OF ONE-OFF MEETINGS

Groups are often based on one very specific problem, but they may find there is an area of overlap between them. They also often find it difficult to invite an outstanding speaker and guarantee a reasonable audience. Here's how four local groups dealt with both issues.

★　Three new groups had grown up at the same time: the Food Allergy Support Group, the Migraine Group and the Asthma Group. They found a common interest in allergies generally, joined up with the Eczema Society, located a knowledgeable, well-known speaker and set up a joint meeting. The cost of publicity and the rent of a large room in the central library was split between them. The large audience of over 100 gained knowledge and the groups enjoyed the contact and working together. All costs were met by donations at the meeting and many new members joined individual groups.

SEEKING EACH OTHER OUT AT OTHER PEOPLE'S MEETINGS

When groups get established, they often find themselves involved in joint activities, relating to, but outside the self-help field. International Year of Disabled People, for example, brought together a wide cross-section of groups. This type of wider contact can be very useful in itself – and also gives opportunities to meet and talk to other self-help groups. No organization or planning is needed, just an awareness that they may be kindred spirits.

You can seek them out without too many problems, even a brief conversation can bring surprising results.

★   The Partially Sighted Society and the Eczema Society both took part in a display put on by the local Council for Voluntary Service. The organizers had helped by putting their display boards close together and in the inevitable lulls during the day, members enjoyed talking. They both picked up a few hints and said how much they'd appreciated contact.

JOINT MEETINGS OF GROUPS IN THE SAME BUILDING

You may be like ships that pass in the night – you meet in the same building but on different evenings and never see each other. But you may have a common interest, you certainly all are familiar with the meeting place. Would an occasional get together be helpful?

★   An imaginative GP welcomed neighbourhood based self-help groups using the meeting room in the health centre. The number of groups grew, with sensitive support from the health centre staff, and he suggested trying out a joint meeting. It proved useful practically – and also gave a neutral friendly place for groups to talk about their relationship with professional workers and to identify weaknesses and strengths in their own groups.

Contact and joint activity where there's outside back-up

Most group members want to put most of their time into their own group. But if an outsider can do some of the organizing and provide resources, groups can enjoy and benefit from a wider and more ambitious range of activities. The outsiders could be local professionals. A health visitor for example, might know of a number of small groups for parents of handicapped children, and help them get together and arrange joint activities.

Some towns may have a specialist self-help support project. Many others will have a CVS, a Volunteer Bureau or a Community Health Council who are interested in and supportive to self-help groups. Their resources will be more limited but they too may be able to sponsor and back up joint activity. What has been done?

JOINT PUBLICITY AND INFORMATION

Groups have found that joint publicity and information can be very valuable – it both brings new members in to particular groups and creates an awareness in the community of the existence and value of self-help groups generally.

- In Leicester, groups join together in a monthly self-help spot on the local radio, part of another programme.

- In Hull, a directory of self-help groups was collated and distributed to local professionals.

- In Nottingham, groups give joint talks to trainee doctors and health visitors, and share a monthly column in the local paper.

- A poster was one way of publicizing self-help groups in Northampton.

JOINT MEETINGS

★ 'It seemed to spur us on.' 'It lifts me up each time I go.' 'I love these kind of things – we get to know each other better.' Self-help groups in another town had the opportunity to meet at a series of summer evening discussions. They heard speakers from outside and, even more useful, from people in other groups. People looked in depth at specific subjects in small groups. The local self-help support team made the arrangements and a day centre gave free accommodation. The caretaker had to gently edge them out at 10 o'clock, the lively conversations went on so long.

People don't necessarily want a formal federation, but they do sometimes welcome the opportunity to meet in this way.

JOINT TRAINING COURSES

Are there subjects that you feel you'd like to study for a short time? A short course, set up specifically for members of self-help groups can be valuable.

★ Groups in one area found that many of them were involved in 'counselling', sometimes on the phone, sometimes face to face.

It became more than befriending, and met a need for one-to-one help between group members outside the meeting – but it was a challenging and sometimes difficult technique. A local counselling service put on a five session course in counselling techniques, attended by members of five local groups. It didn't turn them into professional counsellors but equipped them with some skills and increased their confidence.

HELP TO NEW GROUPS

With some outside back-up, it can sometimes be possible for new groups to get help from established groups on a more systematic basis than the odd visit. One experiment in a self-help support scheme showed that a few long-term members enjoy the opportunity to guide new self-helpers.

★   A local trust gave £500 to meet the expenses of what came to be called a 'Supporters' Club'. Six experienced members of self-help groups became involved, meeting monthly to back each other up and get guidance from a community worker. The grant met their travel expenses. They were linked, either individually or in pairs, with people starting new self-help groups, for about four months. Though their individual problems were very different, the supporters proved to be a great boon to those starting off.

The limits to networking

The stories above illustrate the results that can come from 'networks' of self-help groups. But there are limits to networking – you need to be realistic, while recognizing the advantages. What are these limits?

- People's first loyalty is to their own group.

- They are likely to have limited time, energy and resources.

- There's a risk over getting too formal and structured.

- The rich variety of self-help groups means there will only be some common links between them.

- Networks may only work over a short period of time, perhaps focusing on a particular issue of common concern.

In summary

Many local groups may find benefits in taking part in a network of local self-help groups. It can lead to information, support and practical advantages. But there are limits to what can be done, and someone to organize a network may be essential.

Any network should be based on the recognition that groups need to be independent and choose for themselves how and when, if at all, they take part.

Thinking more deeply

Changes as groups grow

Quite a lot is known about changing phases and experiences in groups generally – it's referred to as group dynamics. This guide doesn't attempt to cover the topic from this angle. There are some in-depth books published on group dynamics and group work which your local library will probably have, or you could look out for short courses in your area which may give you more insight. Here are the more practical issues that can affect groups.

Numbers going up and down

It's very common for groups to start with a small core of interested people planning and organizing; then to experience a big upsurge of membership; followed by a dwindling away and then to settle at a modest number. So if membership has dropped after a few months, take heart. 'There were only three of us left', said David, 'and we did get dispirited. But we kept on meeting at my house, took advice from a friendly community worker – and now look at us!'

It's not only feeling downhearted that's the problem. If you have to find a regular sum to pay the rent for each meeting, it can be very hard to keep going when attendances are small. And if you ask a speaker, it can be very embarrassing when only five people turn up – although you probably mind more than the speaker does.

And what should you do about people who seem to have stopped coming? Do you chase them up with letters, phone calls or visits? It could feel intrusive – people stop coming for all sorts of reasons.

Or they could feel very touched that the group cares about them.

It's a difficult issue to tackle but there are ways of dealing with the situation:

- Get donations from people when attendance is large, in case attendance drops and you need the money.

- Keep going in a modest way – perhaps moving into a smaller room in the same building.

- Ask owners whether they will give you a rent-free period till you get over the hump.

- Warn any speaker that numbers may be small.

- Consider continuing to communicate with past members, maybe by a newsletter or duplicated sheet, at least for a time, until it seems certain they are not returning. They may otherwise assume that the group has folded up.

- Concentrate on the needs of those of you who've stayed.

- Work together on publicity planning in order to get more members.

You'll probably think of other ways of coping. It's quite a challenge, but don't assume that a drop in numbers means the end of the group – it's all too easy to equate large attendance with success, and that's not necessarily so in self-help groups.

The group decides to split

Groups split for all sorts of reasons:

- Personality clashes

- To focus on specific neighbourhoods

- To concentrate on one particular aspect of work

- Rigidity of the original group

- Sheer numbers

Some of these provide logical reasons for change, others are a response to tension and problems. Whatever the reasons, it won't be a simple process when a group decides to split. I've deliberately used a neutral sounding word to describe the process of one group becoming two. But there are others: the new group can be described as a *splinter, breakaway,* or *alternative* group. These names suggest that splitting is not always comfortable – and it can indeed be painful.

It may be particularly difficult when resources are involved. Do you divide the bank balance equally? Who gets the filing cabinet? There's that wonderful volunteer who provides transport – will you be fighting over her? Here are some ways of dealing with difficulties:

- Talk openly and frankly, and use the group to share the problems.

- See the split as a positive move, a challenge, an opportunity for growth and for more people to undertake responsibilities.

- Draw in a neutral person if that might help.

- Don't get too hung up about money and resources.

- See the well-being and happiness of all of you in the long run as your overall objective.

Too many members

Splitting is one solution to this problem. Setting a limit on numbers in your group is another. It can be absolutely right for a group to restrict membership, and indeed some groups have proved to be more effective as a result. But this can be painful too if you have to reject someone who needs the group – how do you tackle that?

There may not be an easy solution, but you can suggest that they start another group. You could consider the following:

- Encouraging people to set up a sister group. It might be in another neighbourhood, or on a different night of the week in the same area.

- Getting several of your members to go along to the new group for a while to give them support. Avoid competition.

- Telling people about local organizations or individuals who might help them start a new group.

- Learning from the experience of Alcoholics Anonymous. Over the years, they have learnt a great deal about splitting. Their literature, or a talk to a member, may be very helpful.

Lastly, you could consider changes in your group that allow big numbers to be a possibility:

- Spending at least part of the meeting in small groups in separate rooms in the same building.

- Changing the organization of your meetings.

- Meeting more frequently.

Differing lengths of membership

Self-help groups vary considerably in how long people remain members. If they are based on conditions like having a mentally handicapped child, people are likely to remain members for maybe 20–30 years. MENCAP groups are often long-established, well-run organizations, with an experienced, stable membership. But consider a new parent, facing all the problems of a newly born mentally handicapped baby. What do they have in common with parents, maybe now elderly themselves, caring for a mentally handicapped middle aged adult? Is it possible for one group to meet the needs of both sets of people?

In the same way, someone who experienced a stillbirth may go on being a member of a group years after the event. A newly bereaved parent could have very different needs. Former carers of elderly parents may need mutual support to cope with the loss of their parents and the subsequent change in life style. Can the same group meet the needs of current carers? The following is from *Self-help and social care: mutual aid organisations in practice*, Ann Richardson and Meg Goodman, Policy Studies Institute:

★ 'I imagined that all the members would be women of about middle age who were caring for an elderly parent and we would all swap little stories and help each other,' said one member. Instead she found 'a lot of old dears who are desperate to latch on to anything to fill their lonely moments . . . they seem to be of more use to the older woman who is free'.

It's complicated. But there are some ways of dealing with this issue:

● Recognize it and bring it out in the open.

● Maintain a sufficient mix of members.

● Encourage the establishment of sub-groups to meet particular needs.

● Provide a range of activities, which allows choice in the way members are involved.

● Make use of a variety of methods of communication.

● Appoint a young chairperson, who can relate to the needs of new members.

● Consider having separate groups for different age groups.

Changes in objectives

In Chapter 3 it is suggested that it can be very valuable to set yourself: overall goals, specific objectives and priorities. You probably at least work to a generally agreed set of objectives. As groups grow, it's possible for there to be a shift – perhaps unconscious – in what you are trying to do. Change can be beneficial: sometimes groups can become stuck if they don't alter what they are doing.

But if the change is a bit muddled, it can be confusing and bring difficulties. For example, new members may come to a group after reading its literature, expecting a particular form of help and be disappointed, even distressed when it has been superseded by other activities.

★ 'I went to the group for help in dealing with my skin condition,' said Karen, 'and all they wanted to do was talk about the next jumble sale'. She never went back. The group's literature said they provided support. In fact, it had turned into a fund-raising group.

Evaluating your work can be a helpful way of clarifying how objectives have changed. There are other ways of dealing with this issue:

- Use an AGM to undertake a simple review of the past and to discuss priorities for the future.

- Rewrite your leaflets and posters if you have made substantial changes to your objectives.

- Issue a press release (a good excuse for some publicity) about the way you have changed.

This need not be a heavy enterprise – but you should be alert to the fact that groups' work does change, and it's best to recognize this. See it as a positive, healthy development rather than a problem.

Becoming an employer

Most self-help groups are run by people acting as volunteers – they don't get paid. A few groups offer a key officer a small honorarium. But some groups face the change that comes from employing a worker. Here's a story about a Parents Anonymous branch.

★   PA, a group for parents experiencing problems with their children, became very successful. The volume of need, the use made of their services and the good co-operation with professional workers all led to a thriving group. Its administration though, became a major problem. With the help of social workers, the group evolved a plan to appoint a part-time paid administrator. The social services department, after long discussions, made a grant. The social workers helped the group with the process of appointment, and to tackle the issue of whether an outsider could apply. (It was agreed it should be an internal appointment). The CVS provided an office and offered to process the salary. The worker has increased publicity, recruited more active members and organized training, while the group itself continues to be responsible for its work overall.

A success story: but be wary, it's not always a simple move. Look at this checklist, and read the books in the booklist on pages 144–5. Be particularly cautious about taking on a worker for 12 months or so, whether from Manpower Services Commission or elsewhere. It takes a long time for a worker to become effective and self-help groups need continuity. Short-term posts need to be geared to work that can be done in a short time – a research exercise for example.

CHECKLIST

- Will having a paid worker bring problems as well as advantages to the group?

- What funds are available to pay salaries?

- Can you take on the legal responsibilities of becoming an employer?

- What advice can you get from outsiders?

- Is one year or short-time funding possible?

- Can you plan a shared office base so that a single worker is not isolated?

- How will you select a worker?

Becoming an organization that provides services

Some groups begin as mutual support groups, and change to being organizations that provide services. If you are still also trying to give mutual support there will probably be tension at times. It will be difficult to meet the needs of members, especially newcomers who want to share problems, at the same time as managing resources. You will probably be faced with the problem that people will use your services, but not be willing to take a share of the work.

On the other hand, you may be providing a valuable service that no one else will do. You may be tapping unused resources. And you may be acquiring yet another set of skills and knowledge.

Ways of approaching this type of change include:

- Acknowledging that you are now a different sort of group.

- Welcoming it as a positive development.

- Making sure there is still room for mutual support.

Becoming a registered charity

This can take a long time. It may challenge your staying power, rather than your ability to cope with difficult situations! Groups with a national parent organization should have less difficulty in taking this step. You may be able to adopt a model constitution wholesale, and get guidance from the national body.

For more informal groups however, becoming a registered charity is a bigger step. Briefly, the advantages that come from it are:

- It may help you get money.

- It may increase public and professional confidence in you.

- For groups with large incomes and premises, there will be tax and rate relief.

The disadvantages may be:

- The time it can take to achieve, if you are starting from scratch.

- The possible restrictions on political campaigning if you feel you need to urge a change in the law.

- The need to adopt a formal constitution and all that that involves.

Ways of dealing with this change are:

- Seek advice (books and addresses on pages 146–8).

- Draw on any local help (a friendly solicitor, a legal advice service).

- Use other people's constitutions as a model.

- Allow plenty of time.

It is not essential for you to take this step, but it may be right for you, especially once you are established.

In summary

- Most groups will experience some sort of change – sometimes predictable, sometimes not.

- Change should be seen as a positive force, even if it brings uncomfortable, even painful, situations with it.

Ending a group with dignity

Ending a group may be a surprising subject to find in a guide to starting and running them. But stopping a group can be a taboo subject which people find difficult to air. And there is a hidden assumption that if something ends, it must be a failure. It's not necessarily so. It can actually be a brave, positive step. Consider these ways which may help you end a group with dignity, and a sense of achievement.

Self-help groups come and go

It's a fact of life that not all self-help groups are permanent. Over a year, maybe 5–10 per cent of groups in an area will come to an end. This is one of their features which makes them different from more established voluntary organizations. It's not unusual for groups to end.

Some groups are more likely to close than others – it depends to some extent on the problem on which they are based. If it's caring for a handicapped child say, people are more likely to remain as members so that the group is stable. But if the common factor is a temporary change in your life, you'll probably only stay in the group for a while and the whole group is also more likely to disband. It can be better to close in a sensible, organized way if the need for a group has passed, rather than to continue beyond the end of its useful life.

Why do groups come to an end?

There are lots of possible reasons for ending and groups may close for one or more of them. Here are a number of examples from groups that have ended.

- Members *got better*. They had benefited from the group, but found they could now draw support from friends, family and community groups.

- The people starting the group agreed from the beginning only to meet for a set number of meetings – 10 or 20 say – and then to disband, rather like an evening class. It's called a *time limited* group.

- The group was set up as an *experiment* from the start – it was a try-out, and the people concerned decided not to continue it.

- The *need for a group passed*. Professional treatment or research made real progress and people found they could cope.

- The group met the needs of a stable number of people, but did not seriously attempt to bring in new numbers. When members left, the *group just faded away*.

- The group depended on one or more *key charismatic figures*. When they left, the group fell apart dramatically.

- A heavy-handed *national organization* made the local branch close, because it wasn't fulfilling the conditions under which they asked their local branches to operate.

- *Personality conflicts* led to people leaving and the group became unworkable.

- The intrusion of strongly held *religious beliefs* into what appeared to be a neutral group brought too much tension.

- *Just too many things against* it – a combination of personal illnesses or pressures; opposition from professionals; apathy; lack of a meeting place and resources; members spread out over a wide area.

- The group presented an *uncomfortable challenge* to the community, for example women, who had previously stayed at

home, came into public view, so leading to disgreement with
their husbands; or the issue on which the group was based
aroused hostility and proved unacceptable.

Is it possible to make ending a better experience?

The list above begins with a number of quite acceptable reasons for
ending a group. It should not take much to come to terms with its
closure if the reasons are straightforward and understandable. In
fact, closing can be a very positive step, leading to other
developments. But further down the list, the possible situations are
less comfortable. It's almost bound to be difficult and a certain
amount of feeling of failure may be inevitable. These are
suggestions of ways which may help ending a group to be a better
experience.

- *Accept* that ending a group is not unusual, and don't feel a
  great burden of guilt about it.

- *Bring in* a supportive outsider to help you think through your
  decision, if that would be helpful. Some groups need to be
  reassured that they are doing the right thing.

- *Evaluate* what you have achieved while you were in existence.
  What have individuals gained from the group? What have you
  done to educate the public about your problem? Make a short
  list of questions and discuss them together.

- Have a *final meeting*. It's sometimes easier to accept the loss of
  something if you have a ritual to go through, an event that
  marks the end. Even if it's just a handful of members, it may
  help to meet formally for the last time. People may want to say
  things they'd not been able to voice before.

- *Publicize* your ending if you are brave enough. Realistically, of
  course, some groups just fade away. A final meeting, and
  publicity about their closure may not be practical. But if you
  are feeling confident, it may help to tell other people you've
  decided to close.

- Pass on your *resources* to be used in a positive way. Any money
  left in the bank account could help another group send a

member to a conference. A hospital might welcome a plant or a picture – the exact use is up to you.

- *Tie up loose ends* as much as possible.

Ways of preventing a painful ending

It may be inevitable that a group ends, but there are steps you can take early on in its life which will help prevent its closure, if it occurs, being too painful. These suggestions will also be helpful if you are successful and the group flourishes.

- Start by thinking of what you are doing as an *experiment*, which may or may not work – you'll wait to see what happens.

- Agree to meet for a *specific number of meetings*, then review your future.

- Don't let your group be listed in a *directory* of any kind before you are sure of its future.

- *Record* what you do as you go along – minutes, diary, photos, scrapbook, copies of letters. You may be able to leave it with a helpful outsider in case someone in the future starts a similar group. They'll gain from your experience and you'll feel more positive about it.

End with dignity

Self-helpers themselves should be the ones who decide to start a group – similarly you should be the ones who decide to end it. It may be a positive, sensible step and you may have no feelings of guilt or failure. You don't have to feel a failure. If you can evaluate what you have achieved you may find that you've done a lot: there are bound to be some good results.

Realistically though it will not always be a pleasant experience. Perhaps it will help to know that it can be painful and distressing, and that others have gone through it.

In summary

- Self-help groups come and go, for all sorts of reasons.

- Some end because people have got better and they are no longer needed.

- With foresight it is possible for many to end with dignity and a sense of achievement.

- For others it will, almost inevitably, be a difficult experience, but one which they are not alone in facing.

Extending members' skills and knowledge

Many self-help groups aim to equip their members with information about their condition and learn ways in which they can cope with it. This chapter looks at the need for more knowledge about jobs within self-help groups rather than this aspect.

It's a good idea for members of self-help groups to join in and work together, but does it actually always work that way? A study of four sets of local groups – all with formal, committee-type structures – found that it was common for a few hard-working members to shoulder most of the jobs. And while there was a lot of mutual help, it wasn't always give and take at the same time. Instead, people tended to become the givers of help as they themselves began to cope better. It's easy to have a rosy picture of a self-help group: people all participating, and all helping each other at the same time.

But realistically, this doesn't always, or even often, happen. Most people join groups just to meet their own needs. But many of them go on to give a lot of help, both to the group and to each other, often surprising themselves and other people.

★ 'There was this woman in our group,' said Bill, 'she came week after week, sat there mute as a maggot. Suddenly one week she produced three policemen who did a sponsored climb and raised £1000 for us!'

Yet others will only take help from the group and then leave without really having put anything into it.

Does your group have untapped potential?

Are there people in your group who might join in a bit more, if only certain barriers were lifted? There is often a lot of untapped potential among people which never gets released. Can you think of anyone? Are there things that you might do if only ——? Or are there jobs you cheerfully take on now, which a year ago you couldn't have faced? What helped you over the hurdle so you could do them?

What stops people joining in?

Lack of confidence

It's very common for people in self-help groups to suffer from a lack of confidence – an illness may especially be a contributing factor.

Lack of experience

'I've never done anything like this before!'

Fear they can't do the job

'I just don't know how you deal with the job of being secretary – I don't think I could ever do it.' People may well be ready to help in principle, but hold back from fear of not knowing what to do, or how to do it.

Cliques

Any group of people, not just a self-help group, can get too cosy. The positive, supportive side of close relationships is good. But if a clique is too firmly installed, it is difficult for new people to feel welcome, and members are even less likely to offer to help.

Over-formal structures

Structures are needed in groups, but they should be tools which make it work, not barriers to involvement. Formal organization can stop people joining in, particularly in large groups.

Low turnover in office holders

One group for parents of handicapped children recognized this difficulty and now has a rule that no one can hold office for more than three years. It's easy for a few willing horses to continue to take the lead, and for the rest of the group to let them.

Poor record keeping

One reason for people continuing in office may be that all the records are in their head, or maybe in a drawer in their sideboard. No one else then feels they have the necessary background knowledge to take over the position.

Health problems and caring obligations

Some of the problems on which self-help groups are based are immense. It's not surprising that some people simply haven't the time or energy to help anyone else, or to take on jobs in the group. This happens particularly if they can never predict when they will be available.

No time to learn

Have you ever tried letting a child cook a meal? It takes twice as long, there's an awful mess and the result may not be perfect. But the immediate feeling of satisfaction for you both is immense, and in the long term, it's a step to acquiring greater skills. But it needs time and the adult must hold back – it's the same in self-help groups. Allowing someone else to learn needs time and patience but it's worth it in the long run.

Cultural and class barriers

Some people come from a background with a tradition of joining in and taking responsibility. To others it's a new idea. Barriers of class, sex and race may prevent some people from full participation.

Getting over some of these problems

Here are some reminders of ways you can run a group which should help participation:

- Have a structure that encourages people to join in
- Sit in a circle at meetings
- Create the opportunity for long-serving members to act as examples, and as befrienders to newcomers
- Share out jobs
- Have a range of activities
- Be selective in what help you accept from outside
- Communicate with each other effectively

Encouraging people to join in

Not everyone will take on tasks in a self-help group. Perhaps it helps to accept this from the start. But there may be other ways of making it more likely that they will join in. Two other factors might be stopping people from joining in: lack of confidence and a feeling of inability or inadequacy.

Both these are often great obstacles for people to overcome. They may never scale them like an Olympic hurdler, but with a bit of practice, and a shove from some friends, they may scramble over.

It may not only be a particular illness or disability that saps people's confidence. The experience of being a patient or a client can, sadly, contribute to this. It's perhaps not a coincidence that a majority of members of many self-help groups are women, and that there has been an upsurge in the number of groups based on problems particularly relevant to women. Women are often much less confident about their skills and potential than men. And caring for others, or coping with a severe illness or disability keeps you away from your community. If you are at home all the time, your opportunity to mix is limited and your confidence level can easily go down.

If you are lacking in confidence, you may think you can never do a job – the two are closely linked. But there's more to it than just that. Many people in self-help groups come new to the whole business of organizing and have never had the chance to pick up relevant skills. It's not an easy task to start and run a self-help group. If you are really serious about encouraging people to join in, you must provide opportunities for them to learn new skills and extend their abilities.

Putting it into practice

Some groups have found the following ways have helped them to extend members' skills and knowledge.

RUNNING COURSES

Training sounds rather grand, putting on a short course is perhaps a more comfortable way of describing it. Or calling it a series of discussion evenings may get people to come when they would never dream of 'going on a course'. Whatever you call it, short courses do seem to help people over the twin barriers of confidence and competence.

★   DIN – a group for sufferers of tinnitus (Darned Infernal Noise) – uses a telephone link. It has one number which is intercepted by the operator, who then tells the caller the telephone number of the member who is taking calls all that month. It's a challenging job to take on, and it fell to a few committed members, until they set up a short course. This included listening skills and other useful topics – but it also gave the opportunity for people to share their experience of doing such a taxing job, and to support each other. It made all the difference and many more members now take a turn.

It may also be fruitful to join up with the other self-help groups for joint courses, or to go on outside courses, such as those put on by the Workers' Educational Association. For a first step, however, people will probably feel safer in their own surroundings, and with people they know. A local adult education centre or community college may be able to advise you how to go about it.

While people don't need training to be members of self-help groups, education on a modest scale like this can be immensely useful.

GOING IN PAIRS

★   'You don't mind us both coming do you? You see, we've never done it before.' A new branch for parents who had experienced a cot death was anxious to make links with health visitors. An invitation to speak to their training course was very welcome – but also intimidating. Janet and Laura prepared their talks together, shared their anxieties and found their way round the building. Their joint talk was outstandingly successful.

Another group, who now make a practice of giving talks to professional workers plan so that one experienced speaker and one new speaker go together.

It's not only giving talks that this can apply to. You may need to discuss an application for a grant, do an interview at a local radio station or organize a new set of posters. If you build a tradition into a group that a new member normally goes along with one or two long-serving members, you may be surprised how much they learn. They may be much more willing to take on the job next time round, and it's also much more fun.

It's also possible to share formal tasks. Some groups have a post of assistant secretary, for example. That person takes over the following year.

MAKING RECORDS EFFICIENT AND ACCESSIBLE

★   'I've taken on the job as secretary', said Tess, a note of despair creeping into her voice. 'The person I've taken over from brought a carrier bag full of bits of paper round to my house, and it's still sitting in the corner. I can't bring myself to tackle it.' She would, in time, as she'd been secretary to another type of group already, and the actual job didn't scare her. But another, less confident person might have suddenly found a good reason why she couldn't be secretary after all, and just handed the bag on.

★   A group for parents of asthmatic children were having an AGM. The first secretary had done the job well, and would have liked to continue, but her child's health just did not permit her to carry the responsibility any more. Carol, a new member, had seen the well-kept minute book, the file of copy letters and the box of membership cards, and tentatively offered to take over, if she could have a bit of help.

It needn't be too sophisticated, or need vast amounts of money, but having systems for keeping records does help. It makes it possible to ask someone to take on a job, with the tools for doing it already there, rather than have to salvage a muddle.

MAKING IT PRACTICALLY POSSIBLE

'I'd love to help, but you see, I can't leave my mother.' Carers will find it difficult enough to get to meetings, let alone share in the jobs. It's worth thinking about various ways of making it possible. Some practical suggestions are:

●   Providing a sitter from the group, so the carer can join in an activity.

●   Providing transport.

- Having meetings in the house of someone who isn't very mobile.

Being realistic again, it just may not be possible to involve people if their health or caring responsibilities are too great. It may be later on that they become the givers of help.

MAKING NEWCOMERS FAMILIAR WITH ACTIVITIES

Welcoming newcomers is a very important task for any self-help group. Some have special members responsible for doing so. Newcomers may join in order to be useful while others will only offer help later. Whichever is the case, unless a new member knows exactly how to be useful, they may never volunteer.

To give a practical example, if you know where the kitchen is and where the drying-up cloths are kept, you're much more likely to offer to wash up the coffee mugs. It may be just on that level that people want to participate at first.

Equipping people with knowledge about where things are and how things are organized right from the beginning also establishes that everyone in the group is expected to help. This may not be straight away but the expectation is there if the seed is sown at their first meeting.

Be realistic

In practice not everyone will want to join in. Some groups run happily with a mother figure; or depend on a few people with time to spare who desperately need to feel needed. And personal pressures may severely limit participation.

But be on the lookout for untapped potential and find ways of releasing it. It is possible to extend members' skills and knowledge with a little thought and some modest resources.

In summary

- Recognize barriers
- Familiarize newcomers

- Have helping structures

- Give practical help

- Set up courses

- Keep records

- Do things in pairs

Campaigning for change

Do you think of yourself as a pressure group? Some self-help groups, including groups based on anonymity, decide that they will not be involved in any activity that involves comment on services or in promoting change. Other groups are based on an issue which means that campaigning for resources and a change of attitude is the core of their work. In between come groups – probably a majority – who see mutual support as their main objective, but also wish to take up issues and campaign for change.

Another book in this series, *Citizen Action* by Des Wilson, will be useful for a more detailed look at this type of work. But it's valuable too to see how campaigning can be a natural objective for some self-help groups, and how it interweaves with other activities in others.

Members of self-help groups are often well-placed to contribute to discussions on resources and policies. They are 'informed consumers'. But how do you feel – as an individual – about feeding back your opinion, maybe a critical one, to professional workers in the health and social services? Probably uneasy. You may depend on them for care and services, and you probably appreciate what they do for you and your family. An individual will find it hard to do. A self-help group can comment more easily.

Why might you choose to campaign – and for what?

There's a variety of reasons why groups choose to work in this way. This checklist may help you think it through:

CHECKLIST

- Is there a desperate need for particular services for members of the group and their families?

- Do you want to campaign on behalf of all people experiencing the problem, and to increase services and resources so everyone benefits?

- Do you see a need for change in the way services are provided and organized?

- Do you want a big increase in resources?

- Do you see a need for more co-operation between different departments or professions?

- Do you want consumers of services to be more involved?

- Do you want to educate the public about your condition?

Groups could be campaigning for:

- Particular new services

- More resources

- A change in organization

- Better co-operation and joint planning

- A change in public opinion

What will people think of your action?

With many conditions, there is likely to be a lot of public sympathy and support for groups who press for better services. Groups based on a condition that attracts less public approval, often already feeling stigmatized, may find it a harder battle to win support for their campaigns.

Professional workers are likely to be ambivalent in their attitudes. Many of them will welcome attempts to increase resources and improve services – it's what they may well be trying to do too. In this case, you should be able to work in harmony, as a team. Some campaigns, however, challenge professional services: groups running them will be seen as trouble-makers.

Professionals tend to be very possessive about their job and their skills. Your campaign may be asking them to share knowledge and prepare policies jointly, so they may feel threatened. Some could also fear they might lose their jobs if far-reaching changes were made. And it is never easy to accept criticism.

There will be approval and sympathy, but there will also be opposition and tension. You are likely to be walking on a tight rope between the two.

A job for the whole group?

★   A Home Births Support Group was started by a group of women who had been able to have their own children at home, and were very committed to the idea of women being able to choose where to have their baby. While recognizing that some births are safer in hospital, their research showed that many are just as safe at home. Their group focuses on efforts to make home births an option and so for services to be easily available. While also giving each other support, their group is centred on a campaign.

In this case, the whole group – which has a small membership – is involved in working for change. Though it needn't necessarily be so. Some groups find it works well for a small sub-group to be responsible for pieces of work, and people who are particularly interested in this aspect of a group's work can become involved as they wish. This avoids the problem of pressing people to be active when they just need support for their own situation.

How can you achieve change?

Campaigning may involve specific action, and it can also be interwoven among a variety of self-help group activities.

MOUNTING AN ACTIVE CAMPAIGN

●   A branch of the Schizophrenia Fellowship mounted a campaign for a day centre, even demonstrating at County Hall.

- A group of parents of children who sniffed glue collected 500 signatures on a petition asking for a ban on glue sales, and presented it to their MP.

- A branch of the Eczema Society wrote to head teachers, sending them literature about eczema, offering to come and talk and clarifying issues like children swimming.

INVITING SPEAKERS

Groups have found that inviting speakers has two-pronged success. They learn from the talk, but it also gives them an opportunity to feed back experiences and educate people in positions of authority. Groups have successfully invited consultants, councillors and members of health authorities with this aim.

FUND-RAISING FOR EQUIPMENT

Quite modest fund-raising efforts can provide equipment that changes the way services are provided. A stillbirth group for example, influenced the care given to parents by the resources such as the parents' room, that it provided for the hospital. An asthma group helped prevent hospitalization by equipping GPs with nebulizers. For this to be successful, there must however be co-operation and trust, and it's as well to involve the professionals concerned in planning what you do.

TAKING PART IN FORMAL CONSULTATIVE BODIES

There are increasingly more opportunities for consultation and participation in decision-making through formal bodies. What these are will depend on where you live. Community Health Councils, (in Scotland, Local Health Councils; in Northern Ireland, District Committees) welcome voluntary groups as members. In England and Wales, Joint Consultative Committees have voluntary representatives too. Some doctors' practices have Patient Participation Associations.

Self-help groups find membership of any of these can be time-consuming and challenging, but it does give opportunities for comment and influence.

DOING SOME RESEARCH

This may sound rather high powered! National organizations are well placed to do this in a sophisticated way but local groups can also find out facts, draw them together and make recommendations. Some have successfully asked students on a social work course to undertake surveys and write reports. Others have had workers for one year through the Manpower Services Commission. This approach gives you hard facts to back your case and deals with the possible criticism that your campaign is not based on real need, but only on the claims of a few vociferous individuals.

SEIZING OPPORTUNITIES AS THEY ARISE

For example:

- Giving a talk to professional workers about your group, and using discussion to feed back comments on *their* work.

- Commenting in the press on reports and news items.

- Responding to requests for comment from consultants on the way their departments' services are organized.

- Talking to officers and members of public authorities whenever you happen to meet them.

Campaign alone – or with other organizations?

Some issues may be so specific that you feel you must pursue them alone, and you may be in a stronger position if you do so. With other issues though, you may be more effective through forging an alliance with other local organizations. They may be other self-help groups; organizations concerned with the same issue; or an umbrella body of some kind. This will help prevent isolation, share out the jobs and make it easier to meet the costs.

Sometimes an unexpected ally can appear, and even take over a campaign for you – the local paper or radio station has often proved to be a more effective campaigner than the group that started it all off. Don't despise such an offer.

For groups with a national organization, there is also the option of alerting them to a need, and asking them to take action. This could be very appropriate for a national issue but won't take care of any need for local change.

However you plan to put on pressure, you may want to draw on outside sources of help for advice. For example, you may need to know the structures of public authorities and the right timing for a campaign. It's no good trying to bring about change when an irrevocable decision has been made. Organizations like a CHC or CVS may be very useful.

Is this playing politics?

It's not party politics – something self-help groups should avoid – but you can't escape the fact that in campaigning you *are* being political. You are contributing to debates on policies and to decisions on resources. You are influencing public opinion and asking for change.

It's not politics in the sense of Conservative, Labour, Liberal or SDP, but it is politics in a general sense. Not all groups will choose to work in this way, but there is no need for those who wish to do so to hold back.

What might the benefits be?

- You may achieve the changes you set out to get – and receive credit for your action.

- You may see other people do what you suggested, but have to hold back your natural protests that it was your idea. You will still have achieved your objective.

- You may get more members – campaigning usually results in useful publicity.

- It may help members feel their life has more purpose – at least they are doing something.

And, as in so many self-help group activities, you will find that people will grow in confidence and skills.

In summary

Campaigning for change is not a form of activity for all self-help groups. Decide among the group whether you have the resources and the motivation to become a campaigning group. If you do, you are in a strong position to feed back members' experience and make comments. There are many ways of interweaving campaigning with other activities.

A welcome to all?

Members of a self-help group are the people who decide who can join – and who can't. You are bound to set limits to your membership. You will be excluding some people. Here are some examples:

- A group for women coming off tranquillizers excludes men with tranquillizer problems.

- A group for divorced Asian women excludes other divorced women.

- A group for working adults with hearing loss excludes young, old and unemployed deaf people.

- A sickle cell anaemia sufferers group excludes people with white skin, as the condition only affects people with dark skin.

- A group for parents of handicapped children in a particular neighbourhood excludes parents living elsewhere.

There is no need to justify your membership rules – defining who can come is a necessary step in setting up a group, and being precise about it can be a great strength. But you do have to consider two possible obligations:

- To make very clear in your literature and publicity who is entitled to come.

● To deal sensitively with enquiries from people who need help
  but don't qualify for membership.

Does everyone who qualifies feel welcome?

Most groups welcome everyone who has a specific problem and
feels the need to do something about it. Some may also draw
members only from a particular area, and others may also set a
limit on numbers. If people qualify can they join your group?

Do you welcome:

● People from all social classes?

● People with a physical disability?

● Both sexes?

● All ages?

● All religions?

● All ethnic backgrounds?

You may be able to make other additions to this list, and use it to
review your membership. Are there barriers, visible or invisible,
which stop people coming in the first place, or make them feel
unwelcome when they actually arrive?

Barriers to membership

Stairs

These are a practical barrier. Groups based on a physical disability
or a serious physical illness will have thought this through. They
will choose their meeting place with care. But what about other
groups? You can be depressed and handicapped for example. Is it
easy to get into your meeting room and to toilets? Do stairs make it
impossible for anyone who finds them difficult to negotiate to join
the group?

Atmosphere

Both the actual feel of the *place* and the attitude of the *people*. Is
there a pleasant atmosphere in your meeting room? Do people feel

Is your meeting place daunting?

comfortable and welcome, particularly when they arrive for the first time? If not, they may not come again. If the building looks particularly daunting from the outside, with no indication of the group's meeting, some potential members may never make it over the threshold in the first place.

An apparent membership of white people

We live in a multiracial society, though in some rural areas, of course, there may be few people from ethnic minority groups. Many self-help groups working in more mixed areas, based on health problems, seem to have a largely white membership. Does this apply to you? Are you making it possible for members to join from any ethnic group and to feel welcome when they come?

Social class

Groups based in one particular neighbourhood may inevitably attract people from one social class. It may happen naturally that members come from a similar background. But illness, bereavement and disability cut across class divisions and self-help group members come from a variety of backgrounds. Does your group have hidden class barriers? Choice of meeting place; language; arrangements for subscriptions; opportunities for people to join in – these may all make people from some social classes feel excluded.

Transport

The whole question of transport, especially in country areas, is an important one. Does lack of access to transport stop some people coming to your group, and allow others who have transport and are probably better off and less isolated to benefit? It may be very difficult to cope with arranging transport yourself, but consider whether lack of transport may be another barrier.

Fear of gossip

A member of Gamblers Anonymous (GA) travelled 80 miles to go to a meeting of GA in another town. The need for anonymity will vary according to what your problem is, but any group could benefit from the rule: 'What you find in this room, leave in this room.' Is it a tradition in your group that people may speak frankly, knowing that what they say will not be passed on? Do new members understand this from the beginning? It's important for people to feel they can speak openly and in complete confidence.

Sex barriers

It's likely that groups will attract one sex more than the other, and there's almost bound to be an imbalance. There's nothing wrong in that, but if you are open to either sex, do both men and women feel equally welcome and involved?

Ways to lift the barriers

It will depend on your group, but some of these traditions may lift barriers – or stop them appearing in the first place:

- Meeting in a room with good access.

- Putting up posters and signs to show the way to the meeting.

- Providing phone numbers for information about membership and meetings.

- Organizing a creche for young children.

- Providing activities in another room for people members are caring for.

- Helping with transport.

- Ensuring confidentiality.

- Caring for newcomers.

- Involving people from minorities in your membership in positions of leadership and welcome.

- Making sure both men and women undertake jobs.

Special efforts to make yourselves open

Special efforts may help you be more open, and let people know you welcome new members. These could be one-off meetings or efforts, or directed at a particular group of people.

ORGANIZING OPEN MEETINGS

People may want to have a look at you before they join. Professional workers could find it helpful to go along to a meeting of a group before recommending it to a particular individual. Holding an occasional open meeting, maybe only once a year, meets both needs. Or you can welcome people to sit in on an ordinary meeting, as many AA groups allow regularly. Or you can organize a special day, perhaps with a video or a speaker.

LIAISING WITH PROFESSIONAL WORKERS

Professional workers often hold a key to membership. They may be the only people who know of all the people with a particular problem, and so can tell them about the group. You may find it fruitful to make special efforts to inform professional workers about your group. These could include going to them, asking them to come to you, producing literature and so on. It's hard work, but may lift some of the barriers to membership.

LIAISING WITH ETHNIC MINORITY UMBRELLA GROUPS

If your group has a largely white membership, you may like to consider whether you could liaise with umbrella groups for particular ethnic minority groups – Indian, Irish, Polish, West Indian, Pakistani, Bengali and so forth. Many cultural groups in big cities have clubs and community centres, certainly organizations. Could you usefully send them your literature? Get it translated into other languages? Go and give talks? It's all too easy to get into a comfortable racial rut. It's up to individuals whether they come or not, but you may need to make special efforts to make sure a range of people know about your existence and feel they will be welcome.

In summary

- Self-help groups decide on their own membership, which will mean leaving some people out. Make it clear who can come.

- Recognize visible and invisible barriers to membership.

- Evolve traditions.

- Make special efforts to help lift the barriers.

Evaluating your work

Self-help groups of all kinds are growing rapidly in number. But just because something exists, does it work? To some extent, self-help group members vote with their feet. If a group is not meeting their needs, they stop attending. But rather than getting the message through a big drop in membership, you might like to assess your work.

Is your group effective? Is it possible in an organization like a mutual support group to measure effectiveness anyway? How might you do it?

Why might you do some evaluation?

- Groups *change*. Members come and go and their needs change. Most groups need to take change into account.

- What *resources* do you have – and could you use more? Evaluation helps you look at your resources, decide whether you are using them efficiently, and maybe whether to seek more.

- Your group will have *aims* – set out in writing or based on general agreement. If you decide to evaluate what you are doing, you can go back to your aims and see if you have fulfilled them.

- When your group started, what was the exact *original problem* around which it was formed? You may need to dust it off, redefine it or decide whether it is still as true today as it was then.

- Lastly, although evaluation may challenge you and even make you feel uncomfortable, it also allows you to measure *achievements*.

Who are you doing it for?

- *Yourselves*. Your group was set up to meet your own needs and those of people experiencing the same problem. First and foremost you will want to measure your work, and the way you do it, for yourselves.

- *Supporting organizations*. If you are an organization with a formal structure, and maybe are a branch of a national body, you are likely to be getting outside help. You will find that supporting organizations will be more likely to go on backing you if they know you assess yourselves.

- *The outside world*. Many groups will want to put over a good image to the outside world. This could be the general public, potential members or organizations which they might be trying to influence. Evaluation helps you put over a clear, accurate picture of yourselves.

Who should do it?

You and your fellow members are best placed to look at yourselves, to do a piece of self-evaluation. You have the experience of membership, the access to information and you can gear the exercise to the needs of the group. It also gets over the problem of confidentiality. Most groups, if they do any evaluation, will probably want to do it themselves.

If your group is small, involve everyone in the evaluation. If it's large, you'll need to think of another way: a simple questionnaire may help or setting up a small working group. Don't assume that the committee are the only ones to take part. In fact, a committee alone assessing a group may simply confirm their way of doing things is right.

Occasionally an outsider may prove to be a useful sounding board. One group found a morning with a sympathetic community worker helped them review their original aims, what their resources were and what they wanted to achieve in the future. Rather than close the group, as they'd feared, they were able to restart, refreshed and with new priorities.

The worker's background knowledge of the group's origins however was essential in this process. If you invite someone in on this basis they should either have some insight or particular qualities which enable them to help you look at yourselves. Be cautious in your invitation and specific about what you want an outsider to do.

Lastly, a neighbouring branch of your national organization, if you belong to one, might be helpful in helping you make an assessment.

What might you look at?

So many benefits of membership of self-help groups are immeasurable. But certain parts of your group's organization can be measured and you can reflect on other aspects of it. This checklist may help you choose what you might evaluate.

CHECKLIST

Topic	*Sample question*
Aims	Are our aims the right ones?
Membership	Are we attracting all the members we could?
Meeting room	Does our choice of meeting room help our group to run well?
Money	Do we have too little/enough/too much?
Transport	Can we do anything about transport. Should we?
Publicity	Who reads our publicity? What effect does it have?
Publications	How readable and attractive are our publications?
Communication	How well do we communicate in our group?
Leadership structure	Who leads the group? Does it work?
National links	What benefits do we/might we get from national links?
Professional relationships	What professionals do we know? Does it help?
Local links	What local organizations do we know? What benefits do we get?
Changes in the group	Has the group changed? How and why?
Developing skills	How many members take on jobs? Can we extend our skills?
Campaigning	Do we campaign, or might we? How and why?
Welcoming everyone	Does everyone feel welcome? Do we exclude anyone?

These are only samples – you'll need to work out specific questions which suit your group.

It may also be helpful to think of how you actually use a list of questions. Here are two suggestions. You could discuss a question in groups of three and then compare answers in the whole group. Or you could duplicate the list of questions with a set of alternative answers beside them for people to tick for example:

Aims	Are our aims the right ones	Yes/No/To some extent
Membership	Are we attracting all the members we want?	Yes/No/To some extent

This method may produce some definite conclusions, but more likely, will identify topics which will need further discussion.

Collect information

Evaluation makes you look back – but if you've nothing to look back over it will not be an easy exercise. It's important, if you can, to build in collection of information right from the beginning. It needn't be elaborate and can be tackled in a variety of ways, planned to suit your group.

You could consider the following:

- *Keeping records of meetings.* These might be formal minutes, typed, duplicated and circulated. Or they could be a short entry in a diary, handwritten and done in turn by different members. Or anything in between.

- *Asking people how they heard about you.* If it's done automatically but sensitively as soon as they make contact, and recorded, you will have an easy way of evaluating your publicity efforts. If no new members mention your expensive posters put up with loving care, is it worth spending time and money on this form of recruitment?

- *Keeping a scrapbook.* Take photos of activities; keep programmes and invitations; cut out newspaper articles or advertisements. These and other material can easily be pasted into a scrapbook – an invaluable method of letting you look back as well as enabling new members to share the past.

- *Keeping a file of second copies.* If you are typing letters, keep a second carbon and file it in date order. It's a simple useful way of recording what's been done, and is easy to review.

When might you undertake evaluation?

It's best to take stock about once a year and for formal
organizations an AGM provides an opportunity to do so. But it may
be better to choose another time – evaluation is not the same as an
annual report. You may need a special time for this, in addition to
an AGM. You could consider doing it every six months, if a year
seems too long.

Some groups, particularly when they are new, may find it helpful
to build in small pieces of evaluation every few months. It will help
you find out what you want to do and the best way to do it before
you settle to a structure and pattern. Others may suddenly find
themselves at a time of crisis. Taking stock may help you face the
problem and identify ways of dealing with it.

Is there an end result?

A formal piece of detailed evaluation could result in a detailed
written report on what the group feels about itself. A less
structured assessment may only need a few notes. Whatever the
scale, write something down, to be brought out again when the
next piece of evaluation takes place. Another end result may be
change in the group – a new meeting place for example.

Most important, if you evaluate yourselves, you will be able to
count your achievements. Self-help groups have to overcome many
hurdles, and sometimes you may feel the journey you're undertaking is just too hard. Perhaps you think you're running on the
spot, rather than getting anywhere. Evaluating yourselves will
bring satisfaction – you will be surprised at what you've done.

Self-help groups are special. You are one of many people with a
problem doing something for yourself. You are all facing not only
an individual problem, but also the issues that groups have to
tackle. Don't forget you have strength, knowledge and skills – you
are bound to achieve something, and you may achieve a lot.

In summary

Consider evaluating your work yourselves. It will help you reflect
on the past. Count your achievements and plan for the future.

Further reading and reference books

The following books are all recommended for their helpful practical advice on specific subjects. Many are obtainable by mail order. A star ★ beside the publisher's name indicates that an address for buying by post is given in the next section – headed 'Addresses'.

Many of the organizations listed will send you a catalogue of their publications; far more are available than could be listed here.

Finding and running premises: a guide for voluntary organizations. An NCVO practical guide by Judith Unell & Anne Weyman. Published by Bedford Square Press ★ 1985 A very useful book for groups taking on their own premises.

The Community Organizations Survival Kit Published by the National Federation of Community Organizations ★ 1982 All about fund-raising, simply written and full of ideas. Excellent.

How to manage your money, if you have any: an accountancy handbook for community organizations. Published by The Community Accountancy Project but available from NFCO ★ (see above), 1983 A short easy-to-read book, particularly suitable for groups employing a worker or running premises.

Voluntary organizations and the media. An NCVO practical guide by Maggie Jones. Published by Bedford Square Press ★ 1984 Good to dip into for ideas and tips.

144

Get it on radio and television: a practical guide to getting air time.
London Region programmes
by Jane Drinkwater
Published by Pluto Press 1984
Very useful for London groups.

Print: how you can do it yourself
by Jonathan Zeitlyn
Published by Interchange * 4th ed. 1985
A detailed guide to different methods of printing and reproduction.

Working on a committee
by Steve Clarke
Published by Community Projects Foundation * 1978
An entertainingly written, practical handbook, aimed especially at
community groups.

Charitable status: a practical handbook
by Andrew Phillips, with Keith Smith
Published by Interaction (now Interchange *), 2nd ed. 1982
A short, clearly written guide, looking at this complex subject in
detail.

Charitable registration
An information sheet published by The Volunteer Centre, * 1984
Free. Send s.a.e.

Employing people in voluntary organizations An NCVO practical
guide
by Sheila Kurowska
Published by Bedford Square Press * 1984
An invaluable guide for groups taking on staff.

Pressure: The A to Z of campaigning in Britain
by Des Wilson
Published by Heinemann 1984
A detailed guide aimed to help people campaign effectively.

For reference:
National Voluntary Organisations in Scotland 1985
Published by the Scottish Council for Community & Voluntary
Organisations * 1985

Voluntary Organisations. An NCVO Directory 1985/86

Published by Bedford Square Press * 1985
Includes national self-help organizations and many other useful addresses.

The Sunday Times Self Help Directory
Eds. Gillie, Price & Robinson.
Published by Granada Publishing, 1982
A well indexed directory of national self-help organizations.

The Directory of Grant Making Trusts
Published by The Charities Aid Foundation 1985

Addresses

Alcoholics Anonymous
11 Redcliffe Gardens, London SW10 9BQ
Tel. 01-352 9779
Sell literature, provide details of local groups.

Bedford Square Press (the publishing house of the National
Council for Voluntary Organisations)
Publications available by post from
Macdonald & Evans Ltd
Estover Road, Plymouth PL6 7PZ

Charity Commission
14 Ryder Street, London SW17 6AH
for groups in England and Wales based south of a line drawn
roughly from Swansea to The Wash.
& Graeme House, Derby Square, Liverpool, L2 7SB
for groups north of this line

Community Projects Foundation
Publications available by post from
CPF Books
Winslow Press
23 Horn Street, Winslow, Buckingham MK18 3AP

Directory of Social Change
9 Mansfield Place, London NW3
Produces a comprehensive range of publications, particularly on
fund-raising. List can be sent.

Interchange (formerly Inter Action Centre)
15 Wilkin Street, London NW5 3NG
Tel. 01-267 9421
A wide range of publications available by post. List can be sent.

MIND
National Association for Mental Health
33 Harley Street, London W1N 2ED
Tel. 01-637 0741
Another good source of publications and information sheets. List
can be sent.

National Association for Patient Participation
Hazelbank, Peaslake, Guildford, Surrey GU5 9RJ
Tel. 0306 730405

National Council for Voluntary Organisations
26 Bedford Square, London WC1B 3HU
Tel. 01-636 4066
Its services include providing information on CVSs and Rural
Community Councils and a wide range of literature. List can be
sent.

National Federation of Community Organisations
8/9 Upper Street, London N1 0PQ
Tel. 01-226 0189
Produces publications aimed at community groups. List can be
sent.

Northern Ireland Council for Social Service
2 Annandale Avenue, Belfast BTZ 3JH
Tel. Belfast (0232) 640011

Scottish Council for Community & Voluntary Organisations
18/19 Claremont Crescent, Edinburgh EH7 4QD
Tel. 031- 556 3882

The Volunteer Centre
29 Lower King's Road, Berkhamsted, Herts HP4 2AB
Tel. Berkhamsted (04427) 73311

Wales Council for Voluntary Action
Llys lfor, Crescent Road, Caerphilly CF8 1XL
Tel. Caerphilly (0222) 869224

Index